Best Possible Place, Worst Possible Time

Also by Barry Sonnenfeld

Barry Sonnenfeld, Call Your Mother

BARRY SONNENFELD

Best Possible Place, Worst Possible Time

True Stories from a Career in Hollywood

BOOKS

New York

Hachette Books
Hachette Book Group
1290 Avenue of the Americas
New York, NY 10104
HachetteBooks.com
Twitter.com/HachetteBooks
Instagram.com/HachetteBooks

First Edition: October 2024

Published by Hachette Books, an imprint of Hachette Book Group, Inc. The Hachette Books name and logo is a trademark of the Hachette Book Group.

The Hachette Speakers Bureau provides a wide range of authors for speaking events. To find out more, go to hachettespeakersbureau.com or email HachetteSpeakers@hbgusa.com.

Books by Hachette Books may be purchased in bulk for business, educational, or promotional use. For information, please contact your local bookseller or Hachette Book Group Special Markets Department at: special.markets@hbgusa.com.

The publisher is not responsible for websites (or their content) that are not owned by the publisher.

Print book interior design by Six Red Marbles, Inc.

Library of Congress Control Number: 2024941637

ISBNs: 9780306832277 (hardcover), 9780306832291 (ebook)

Printed in the United States of America

LSC-C

Printing 1, 2024

Once again,
for Sweetie.

UNDER PROMISE. OVER DELIVER.
THERE'S NO UPSIDE TO OPTIMISM.

Contents

Contents

Contents

Best Possible Place, Worst Possible Time

The Metaphorical Cat

Physicist Erwin Schrödinger devised a thought experiment to illustrate his problem with quantum physics. His idea was to place a metaphorical cat [the best kind] in a closed box with a weapon that *can*, but not necessarily *will* kill the kitty. [It's a tad more complex than that, but let's move on.]

At this moment, Erwin would argue, since the box is closed and we can't see the cat, it is both alive and dead. Until observed, the cat's fate is up in the air.

I won't divulge my preference, but the point is, until something is witnessed it doesn't exist.

There are at least two sides to every story, and in the case of making a film or television show, you can square that by hundreds of participants. The anecdotes I'm about to share are my observations. There are as many different points of view as there are participants—each one with the observer as hero. There is also a universal disconnect between who we believe we are and what others see us as. It is this disconnect that creates absurdity, comedy, and pain.

My suppositions and memories carry no more weight than others'.

I hope, however, mine are funnier.

Resume

CINEMATOGRAPHER
Blood Simple [1985]

Compromising Positions [1985]

Raising Arizona [1987]

Three O'Clock High [1987]

Throw Momma from the Train [1987]

Big [1988]

When Harry Met Sally [1989]

Miller's Crossing [1990]

Misery [1990]

FILM DIRECTOR
The Addams Family [1991]

For Love or Money [1993]

Addams Family Values [1993]

Get Shorty [1995]

Men in Black [1997]

Wild Wild West [1999]

Big Trouble [2002]

Men in Black II [2002]

RV [2006]

Men in Black 3 [2012]

Nine Lives [2016]

Barry Sonnenfeld

TELEVISION DIRECTOR

Maximum Bob [1998]

The Tick [2001]

Pushing Daisies [2007–2009]

A Series of Unfortunate Events [2017–2019]

Schmigadoon! [2021]

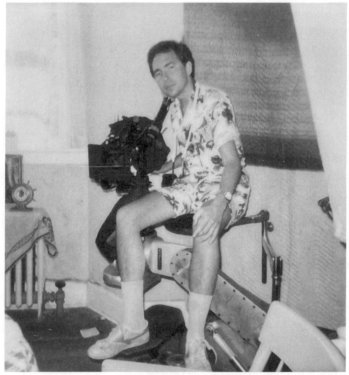

On the set of an ABC After School Special.

A Note to the Reader

Several movies that have been important in my career get short shrift in this book. Films like *Blood Simple*, *Big*, and *Get Shorty* for example, are written about extensively in my memoir, *Barry Sonnenfeld, Call Your Mother*. You should read that book. But since you're already here, start with this one.

Especially Dazzling

Joel Coen, Ethan Coen, and I arrived in Austin, Texas, in 1982 to begin work on *Blood Simple*, the first feature film for all of us. We had not worked our way up any kind of ladder, and not just because I was afraid of heights. By self-declaration, I was a feature film cinematographer, Ethan a producer, and Joel a director. Ethan and Joel had written the script.

Ethan had briefly attended Princeton as a philosophy major but quit via a letter to the dean claiming he had lost his legs in a wood-chipper incident. Or at least, that's what Ethan told me.

What Joel and I had separately learned at film school— I had attended NYU Graduate Film School while Joel was an undergraduate—was to pre-plan everything. Every shot, every edit, was designed before we started to shoot. The worst place to figure things out is on a set, surrounded by the crew biding their time.

By spending as little money as possible on wardrobe, crew, and set building, we bought ourselves as many shooting days as possible. We alternated 5 and 6-day work weeks, and our 42-day shooting schedule was much longer than most low budget films.

Joel and Ethan and I were attracted to stylized movies. Scorsese was a big influence, as was Kubrick, especially his *Dr. Strangelove*. We were also fond of Bertolucci's *The Conformist*.

The Coens and I had lots of creative freedom on *Blood Simple* because we had never worked on a movie and therefore had nothing to lose; we could take big chances with the design and execution of our little film. If we failed, we had no reputation to ruin. We also had no studio thwarting our wacky creative impulses with "notes." This freedom meant we had fun.

In hindsight, I'm amazed directors put up with me as their cinematographer. I was a *big* presence on the set—some might say a *handful*. I had *a lot* of personality. I often wore a stick-on-your-forehead baby thermometer that would glow my temperature. This allowed me to walk up to anyone—Joel, Ethan, Fran, grips, electricians—lean my pinhead forward and ask what my temperature was.

"I've got a temperature!" I would gleefully announce to everyone within earshot.

"What's it at, Ba?" Ethan would yell back.

"Ninety-nine!" I'd scream, holding the back of my hand across my forehead, silent movie actress style.

The film's investors [I think there were about 60] for the most part hated the finished film. They weren't sure if it was a comedy or noir film and didn't grok how it could be both. The boys lugged their finished film around to all the studios, who were happy to look at it since most low budget independent movies were, unlike ours, rarely shot on 35mm film. *Blood Simple* looked like a studio movie with an indie attitude. The studios' production people tended to like it and the distribution teams felt they couldn't market it. After nine months of carrying those heavy film cans around, Joel and Ethan were no closer to finding a distributor. Luckily the boys were able to get the movie accepted at the Toronto Film Festival.

Ben Barenholtz, working for a new distribution company located in Washington, DC, saw the film and liked it. Circle Films agreed to distribute.

The New York Film Festival doesn't usually accept first time filmmakers, nor films that had already been shown at other festivals, but they surprisingly accepted *Blood Simple*.

Our careers changed at around 8 PM on the evening of October 11, 1984, when the next day's edition of the *New York Times* published Janet Maslin's review calling *Blood Simple* "A Black-Comic Romp." Her review begins: "Black humor, abundant originality and a brilliant visual style make Joel Coen's 'Blood Simple' a directorial debut of extraordinary promise." Later she comments, "The camera work by Barry Sonnenfeld is especially dazzling."

I was standing on the corner of Broadway and 72nd Street balancing a Gray's Papaya hot dog [all beef—no bull—three dogs and a drink for $1.85] and the *New York Times* in one hand, a papaya drink in the other. The *Times* had just made me a lauded cameraman.

An interesting side note:

When Danny DeVito hired me to shoot *Throw Momma from the Train*, he shared that viewing *Blood Simple* at their neighborhood movie theater had sent Rhea, his wife, into labor.

Compost

After the *New York Times* review of *Blood Simple*, but before it was released theatrically, I received a call from Pat McCormick, producer of *Compromising Positions*. The film was being directed by Frank Perry, whose previous work included *Rancho Deluxe* and *Mommie Dearest*. The movie was a comedy involving the murder of a philandering dentist played by Joe Mantegna.

Pat had striking blue eyes.

Frank wore old man pants.

Could I send over a VHS tape of *Blood Simple* so they could check it out?

I told Pat the film was very dark, and looking at it on a TV from a VHS tape wouldn't get me the job. I would be happy to rent the Broadway Video screening room in the Brill Building and show them a reel [20 minutes] of the 35mm film but would not send them a video tape.

McCormick said Perry wouldn't schlep to a screening room and I was going to lose any chance of getting the job if I didn't send a tape.

Obstinately, I told Pat thanks, maybe we'll work together another time.

McCormick called back an hour later. If I could book the screening room for the next afternoon, Frank would come over to the Brill Building.

I did, he did, and I got the job.

There's a lesson there.

Compromising Positions, which the crew called "Compost," was a big deal for me. McCormick arranged for my membership into NABET, the more "indie" of the two East Coast motion picture unions. We shot half the film in New York City and the other 50 percent in East Hampton, where I owned a "starter home." The job was fun although it was uncomfortable working with Frank since he had a crush on me and refused to call me Barry, preferring the unfortunate and not accurate nickname "Handsome." He also kept telling me I had beautiful eyelashes, which I admit, is slightly true.

On the set of Compromising Positions.

The lead was Susan Sarandon. Susan was pregnant but didn't want Frank to know. This meant her character mainly wore gray sweats.

"Why would a beautiful woman like Susan Sarandon want to be filmed in sweatpants, Handsome? They make her look dumpy."

"Ya got me, Frank," I said, feigning stupidity.

Susan appeared on *The Late Show with David Letterman* a few days before we started filming. Letterman asked Susan about the film. Did she take roles based on the story or character or the writing? Perhaps the director?

"Ask if they're paying me a lot. That's why I took this one."

A bad start.

I loved working with Raul Julia, cast as a suburban detective. I had the pleasure of directing him in two *Addams Family* movies a few years down the road. The costume designer had given Raul a pair of yellow and brown houndstooth slacks which Raul just loved. Every camera setup he would enthusiastically inquire:

"Barry. Can you see my ponnnts?"

"Yes. Raul. We see them."

"You see my ponnnts? Excellent."

Frank relied on me to design the shots.

One day we were in a cramped kitchen filming a close-up of Raul [no, we could not see his ponnnts].

"What lens do you have on, Handsome?" asked Frank.

"Twenty-seven millimeters, Frank."

"What day of the week is it?"

"Friday?"

"Exactly. We haven't had a really tight close-up all week. Put on the 50!"

"Sure Frank. But the thing is, I can't get the camera any further back, so a 50mm lens is going to be like *an extremely tight* close-up. Like really, really tight."

"Good! It's Friday and I don't want an entire week to go by without a nice tight close-up. We need a shot with some balls!" Frank declared, grabbing a wad of cloth located at the crotch of his old man pants.

"Roger that, Frank. Just one thought: You and I know it's Friday. But when the audience sees the film, they're not going to know what day of the week this shot was photographed. All they'll know is you're cutting to an extreme close-up of Raul Julia saying, 'I'll have an apple.'

"Shouldn't we save our extreme close-ups for lines like 'You killed my husband.' Something slightly more dramatic than a fruit choice?"

"Just do it, Handsome. It's Friday."

"Copy that, Frank."

A Live Action Cartoon

After reading the screenplay of *Raising Arizona*, Joel and Ethan's second movie, I called the boys:

"The film should look like a pop-up book. I'll over-light the foreground so it pops in a three-dimensional way from the background. Almost unrealistically so. Like a fable. Or a live action cartoon. And let's make the camera a character in the film—even more than we did with *Blood Simple*."

Along with *Miller's Crossing*, our eventual third collaboration a few years later, *Raising Arizona* was one of the two films I was most proud of as a cinematographer. They were very different in style. *Miller's Crossing* was my best lit movie. *Raising Arizona* had great self-conscious camera moves.

Joel and I recently joked that if we were shooting *Raising Arizona* in 2024 we would make the same movie at ten times its 1986 cost and it wouldn't be half as good. Same with *Blood Simple*. Back then we used camera techniques we'd be embarrassed to employ now.

For instance, Nic Cage's fever dream: The camera races over a car and fountain, up a ladder, through a window, and into the screaming mouth of Florence Arizona who has just discovered one of her quints has been kidnapped.

If filmed in 2024, we would lay 40 feet of track on which we'd put the longest, most expensive Supertechno50+—a crane mounted on a dolly that has an arm that silently telescopes 37 feet. If you're wondering why a crane with a 37-foot telescoping arm would be called a Supertechno50+, it's because there's another 13 feet of arm behind the post's pivot point that holds all the weights to stabilize this complex device.

The Supertechno50+ would get us over the car, fountain, and up the ladder to the second floor curtained window, at which point, we'd transfer the camera to a dolly and overlap the push through the curtains before heading towards Florence's mouth, adding a lens zoom within the dolly move to get close to her mouth without running her over. By overlapping the push through the curtains on both the crane and dolly shots, we would use that moment to quickly dissolve between the two angles.

Or we might have tried doing the entire shot in one continuous take using a drone.

In 1986, however, the sequence was filmed in a very different, much less expensive way. The first part of the shot was achieved using a two man shakicam. The shakicam is something Joel and Eth picked up from their friend, director Sam Raimi, who used it to great effect in his movie *Evil Dead*.

A shakicam is a 2-inch-wide by 12-foot-long board with a peg on either end for a handle. An Arriflex 2C camera with a 9.8mm Century Optics lens is mounted in the middle of the board, perpendicular to the board's length. The lens' angle of view is so extremely wide you don't need to look through the camera to aim the thing. In addition, because the lens is so wide-angled, it moves through space and changes perspective rapidly, creating a real sense of speed. The 12-foot length of the board, coupled with the wide angle nature of the lens, reduces bumps and foot falls to a minimum. The image seems to float.

Joel and I, holding the board at either end and very low to the ground, ran towards the car and in tandem, raised the shakicam, trying to keep the horizon parallel to the ground. Once we cleared the car, still running, we lowered the camera back down to the ground before lifting it over the fountain, then back down again, finally racing towards the base of the ladder. At this point we tilted the lens towards the sky, lifting the shakicam up as high as possible, skimming the ladder before we cut out of the shot.

During the first rehearsal Joel tripped, slid, and shoveled a dump truck of gravel underneath the skin of his right hand. He was taken to the hospital for painful pebble removal. After that, we always wore gloves. And knee pads.

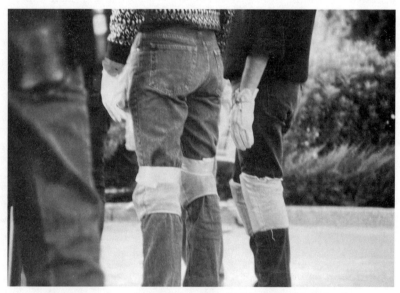

Barry and Joel wearing knee and hand protectors, post Joel's slide.

The second part of the shot used an inexpensive, non-telescoping crane called a "Giraffe" to boom up the length of the ladder, eventually pushing into the open window's curtain. The final segment was perhaps the most difficult. It overlapped pushing through the curtain, then rushed towards Florence, who turns from the crib towards the racing camera as she opens her mouth to scream. We end the shot inside her mouth. The challenge was you can't rush a 420-pound dolly towards a human and stop a couple of inches from their tonsils.

Our solution was to film the shot in reverse—start close on Mrs. Arizona's uvula and as the camera rapidly pulls back, Florence, acting in reverse, turns away from the camera towards the crib that corralled four, instead of five, babies.

The start of the shot, with the lens literally against her teeth, required Mrs. Arizona not to breathe until we started to track away from her, otherwise she would have fogged the lens.

To further complicate the shot, the Coens and I hated opticals—the postproduction manipulation of film footage. Normally a filmmaker would take the piece of film that started inside Florence's mouth and with an optical printer, print it in reverse. But that "optical," until the advent of digital photography, would degrade the image. Our opticals on *Blood Simple* were horrible. What the Coens and I figured out was that if we photographed the shot with the camera *upside down*, starting inside Florence's mouth and pulling back, then flipped the film, so the end of the shot was now the beginning, the image would not only be right side up, but would run backward, or in this case forward, saving an optical. This will be on the final exam, so try to pay attention.

As complicated as this sounds, it was even more difficult since the image on a 35mm piece of film is not centered. There needs to be room on one side of the celluloid for the soundtrack. Whenever the boys and I did one of these upside down to reverse the image trick shots, and there were about half a dozen, you would see Ethan and me sitting on the ground with a piece of paper, drawing a version of a film strip with sprockets on one side only, trying to determine if the camera should be aligned slightly left or right of center. Amazingly, using this low-tech guess work, we offset the image perfectly each time.

A frame from the dolly shot of Florence Arizona discovering one of her babies is missing, origianlly shot upside down and in reverse.

Raising Arizona relied on a very self-conscious, intrusive camera. The use of wide angle lenses and rapid camera moves gave us the wacky energy we were after. I used similar techniques on *Blood Simple*, Phil Joanou's *Three O'Clock High*, and Danny DeVito's *Throw Momma from the Train*.

"Look at me," the camera would practically scream. Perhaps it's because I'm an only child.

I was quite frustrated when the famous cinematographer Owen Roizman called—years later I would hire him to photograph *The Addams Family*. He had been charged with shooting a big, expensive McDonald's commercial and the client wanted it to look exactly like *Raising Arizona*.

"How did you do all those shots?" inquired Owen.

"I'll tell ya, Owen. But I gotta ask: Why didn't they just hire me?"

One man shakicam. POV of fist hitting Nic Cage.

The Baby Pit

There were several reasons we filmed *Raising Arizona* in Arizona— besides that it was Arizona. It had lots of cactuses, always a comedy plus. The state had a "right to work" law, which meant we could hire a combined crew of union and non-union employees. And finally, Arizona seemed to have very lax, perhaps nonexistent child labor laws, which enabled us to build a baby pit.

The movie required five babies—the Arizona quintuplets. All five were often visible in the same frame. Sometimes they were in their crib, sometimes they were crawling. We realized that viewed as a group, the audience wasn't going to fixate on any individual baby, with the exception of Nathan Arizona Jr. Babies kinda look the same. So on a small stage next to our bedroom set, we built a shallow carpeted pit in which we put about a dozen and a half blonde, blue-eyed babies. The parental units sat around in folding chairs reading, knitting, and commenting on how not all the babies were as good as theirs. One mother, desperate to get her little angel picked, reacted in horror when she saw her toddler take his first steps. She kept knocking him down, since we needed crawlers, not walkers. She went so far as to put his baby shoes on backward, hoping that would discourage her precocious, precious bundle of joy from bipedaling, but he was off the picture.

When we were ready for the quints, Joel and Ethan would take a trip over to the baby pit, find five who were awake, and bring them to set. Any baby who cried or made a fuss or just sat slug-like, they'd exchange. No one has ever noticed how many different babies it took to achieve our five "Arizona quints."

Although an adorable baby named TJ played Nathan Arizona Jr., the crawler of our dreams was Cody. He was a combination of excellent actor and supreme stuntman. Cody did about 70 percent of our crawling footage. A real superstar.

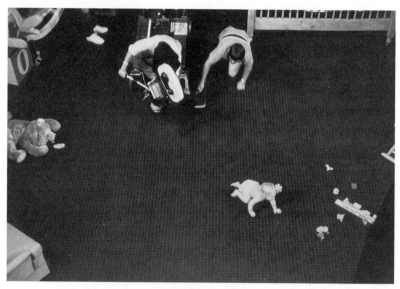

Follow that baby!

Throw Momma

I was hired by Penny Marshall to shoot the movie *Big*. Since Barry Diller, the chairman of 20th Century Fox, wanted Tom Hanks instead of Robert De Niro [Penny's choice], the start date was pushed back more than a half year to wait for Tom. This gave me enough time to photograph Danny DeVito's *Throw Momma from the Train* before returning to *Big*.

Early in preproduction I told Danny we didn't have enough days to film the show with the ambitious camera moves and angles we had planned. The schedule called for 50, and we needed 60.

"Are you a powerful enough director to get us an additional ten days?"

"As a director, I got no power, Ba," said the first time director. "As a movie star, whatever we need, babe," he Cheshire Cat grinned as he rubbed his hands together.

The next afternoon we had 60 days.

A "call sheet" is a piece of paper given to the cast and crew at the end of each day indicating what time and where we were to report for work the next morning. It includes the next day's scenes, any special effects or props that might be needed, the location of the nearest hospital, etc. I had fallen in love with Susan Ringo, who I had taken to calling Sweetie. On *Throw Momma from the Train*, Sweetie was absent. We were dating, but she was in East Hampton with her daughters, Sasha and Amy, prohibited by court order from traveling with her kids more than a hundred miles from New York City, where her estranged husband lived. This not only meant Sweetie couldn't visit me in LA unless there was a long weekend or holiday when her husband had the kids, it also meant I was usually in a bad mood. The cast, director, and mainly the crew, suffered. When Sweetie was a workweek away from a West Coast visit, a new section was added to the call sheet: a map of the United States with a picture of Sweetie in a cartoon car making her way across America. Each day's call sheet would show her imaginary progress.

Danny is extraordinarily self-confident. After attending NYU Film School, retiring from his gig as Mr. Danny, his Asbury Park, New Jersey, hair salon's nom de guerre, he made his way west to Los Angeles in anticipation of becoming a star. As you might suspect, he couldn't get arrested. After a particularly brutal meeting with a casting director where he was told he'd never get an acting job and to find another line of work, Danny told her she was wrong, he was going to be a huge star and stormed out of her office. That evening Danny started his new job as a valet parker at a luxury apartment building in Los Angeles' Wilshire Corridor. The first apartment owner to drop off a car for Danny to park that night was of course that very same casting director.

Somehow, perhaps due to his small role in *One Flew over the Cuckoo's Nest*, DeVito managed to get an audition for the part of Louie, the acerbic dispatcher on *Taxi*, soon to be a hit TV show. He was brought into the audition room where the creators, James L. Brooks, Ed. Weinberger, the Charles brothers, and others sat across from him. Since he had no chance of getting the part, he didn't have much to lose.

"Before we start," Danny barked, "which one of you assholes wrote this piece of shit?"

He was Louie.

Danny became a star.

A slight challenge for Danny, his co-star Billy Crystal, and Anne Ramsey, who played Momma, was the climax of the film, taking place on a train. In retrospect, we should have built a couple of train cars and shot the scene on a blue screen stage, putting in fast moving backgrounds in postproduction. Instead, the crew shot for several days at Magic Mountain, a small, sad amusement park about a 90-minute drive from LA. In addition to a roller coaster and other swell rides, the fun fair also had a dreary train track that circumnavigated the grounds. Unfortunately, the train's top speed was me after my total knee replacement. Since we had our actors chasing each other between cars, the audience would see just how slow we were traveling. I asked the actors to do all their action at half speed, and set the camera at 12, instead of the normal 24, frames per second. Running the camera and having the thespians act at half speed meant, when projected at the standard 24 frames per second, the action would seem normal but the speed of the train, the background, would be moving twice as fast.

Along with *Raising Arizona* and *Three O'Clock High*, *Throw Momma* was my third film in a row photographed with a very wide angle, self-conscious camera. Most of the shots in *Throw Momma* were with a 17.5mm or 21mm lens. There is a specific challenge for actors when filming with a wide lens. To shoot a close-up with these lenses, the camera needs to be very near the actor.

This means that when the on-camera actor looks at the off-camera actor, his or her eye-line is too wide, since the off-camera actor is pushed wide to the right or left of the camera. To keep the actor's eye-line near the axis of the camera's lens, the on-camera actor is asked to look at a piece of tape placed on the matte box, much closer to the lens than the off-camera actor can be. This means the actor is acting to a piece of tape, and not his or her fellow performer.

When Billy Crystal heard I was hired by Rob Reiner to shoot *When Harry Met Sally*, he called.

"Hey, Ba. I'm so excited you're going to do this thing with me and Rob."

"Me too, Billy."

"Just one favor. This is a romantic comedy. I have to look at Meg. I can't be acting to a piece of camera tape stuck to the side of the matte box."

"No worries, Billy. *Throw Momma* was a wacky movie. *When Harry Met Sally* is a handsome romantic comedy. Totally different lenses. You'll be able to look at Meg. I promise."

Billy had gotten so used to my wide angle method of shooting that he called me a few years later from the set of *City Slickers*.

"Barry, the cameraman is using telephoto lenses!"

"Really," I said. "Who is he?"

"Dean Semler."

"He's good," I said.

"But he's not using wide angle lenses. Will it be funny?"

"Sadly not, Billy. Only wide angle lenses are funny. But it will look good."

It actually looked good *and* was funny, so what do I know? *When Harry Met Sally* also was shot with normal lenses and was funny so maybe I'm kinda pedantic about this wide angle lens thing.

Anne Ramsey was wonderful as Danny's Momma. She was recovering from tongue cancer but was up for anything. The only acting she failed at was fake slapping Danny. She could never get the timing right and ended up slapping Danny hard across his face, over and over again.

Years later, Danny spoke at Anne's memorial:

"And I know," Danny proclaimed, "that if Anne is looking down upon us right now, she's saying, 'There goes your fucking sequel, Fat Boy!'"

It's in the Delivery

Both DuArt in New York and CFI in Hollywood were independent film labs that cared about their work and delivered excellent dailies. There were also two larger, more corporate labs that had the high-speed machinery and contracts with the major studios to output most of the industry's release prints. One lab was the excellent Technicolor. The other was the shockingly bad Deluxe— the Yugo of film labs, which had Fox, Orion, Universal, and several other studios as its clients.

"Barry. This is Bud."

Bud Stone was the chairman of Deluxe Film Labs, the Los Angeles based company that was supposed to be printing, but was in fact ruining, the release prints of *Throw Momma from the Train*. It was Deluxe's job to copy the color and exposure of the *Throw Momma* answer print I had supervised at CFI, the film lab that printed the original dailies. Deluxe, once they were able to match the answer print, would make thousands of release prints to be projected in all the US and Canadian movie theaters. The problem was the Deluxe release print, which I viewed in New York at DuArt, the lab I most trusted, was washed out. Bright and colorless.

I was on 54th and Broadway, having just left DuArt when my Panasonic cell phone rang. I placed the body of the phone on the sidewalk, letting the cord between the base and handset uncoil.

"Hiya, Bud."

"Barry. We seem to be having a communication problem."

"You know, Bud. I think what we're having isn't so much a communication problem as a 'Your lab is horrible and I wish I didn't have to use it problem.'"

"Barry. I want to make this right."

"Does that mean you'll let Orion print *Throw Momma* at any place that isn't Deluxe?"

"You know I can't do that."

"Yes you can."

"Well, short of that."

"Bud. Your lab is horrible. I just watched your third try at color timing the movie and the print is so overexposed it looks Edgar Winter in Antarctica during a blizzard."

"Edgar Winter?"

"Albino. Like his brother Johnny."

"In any case," Bud responded, "something must be wrong at your favorite lab because I looked at your movie in the same screening room our timer is using and it looks fine."

"Bud. Believe me. This is not a DuArt problem. And it definitely does not 'look fine.'"

"Barry. I want to make this right."

"So I *can* go to another lab?"

"We already agreed I can't let you do that."

"No we didn't. *You* agreed."

"As I say," sighed Bud. "I want to make this right. So you know what I'm going to do?"

"I give up, Bud."

"I'm getting on the next plane to New York, and I am taking you to dinner. In fact, you choose the restaurant."

"I don't want to have anything to do with you or your lab and now you're forcing me to eat with you? That's how you're going to make it right?"

"You don't want me to come?"

"For the love of God, no."

"I'm just trying to help," Bud groveled.

"Dinner with you is not helping."

"How about this. There's a three-day weekend coming up. Can I fly you out to LA? We'll keep the lab open, you'll sit with the color timer, and you can see what's wrong with DuArt's screening room."

"Sure Bud. I'll fly out. But promise me something."

"Anything Barry."

"Don't take me to dinner."

The Deluxe campus, situated in Hollywood, was a huge factory that smelled like vinegar and looked like Chernobyl.

Chemical spills, rusting film cans, forklifts being repaired. A fetid pool of water in a tunnel. A chain link fence leaning over, praying it would make it through another couple of decades.

"What? And leave show biz?" the fence was thinking.

I was led to the small screening room where Dale, the color timer, had been viewing our movie.

"Water? Coffee?" Dale asked.

"I'm fine."

"Sanka?"

"I'm good."

Dale and I sat together at the console in the back of the room which allowed him to run the film forward and back and communicate with the disgruntled projectionist who had to work on a three-day weekend.

"Before we start," I asked Dale, "how many footlamberts are you getting off the screen?"

"You're asking about footlamberts?"

"Yeah. Did you check?"

"Checked it myself. This morning. Sixteen on each projector."

"Great. Let's get started."

A footlambert is a measurement of the brightness of a projector that's reflected off the movie screen. The SMPTE, Society of Motion Picture and Television Engineers, recommends 16 footlamberts. That is the standard for color timing a print as well as projecting it at your local cinema. The less footlamberts, the darker the image will look.

It is now important to explain the concept of the "silent schmuck."

I was gifted this brilliant observation by Rob Reiner, who I believe got it from Herb Gardner.

A silent schmuck is calling someone a schmuck *silently*, in a passive aggressive manner. For instance, the word "really" can be used as a silent schmuck, as in me saying:

"Stop the projector please," with a Dale response of . . .

"Really? [schmuck]"

Repeating a sentence is also a silent schmuck, as in me saying:

"Stop the projector please," with Dale's response of:

"Stop the projector? [schmuck]"

The movie started to roll. Indeed, it looked very different than what I was seeing at DuArt. Although it wasn't insanely Winters-brothers-bright, it was dull and had no contrast or color saturation.

"Stop the projector please."

"Stop the projector?"—the first of many silent schmucks to come.

"Yeah. Let's stop. And take the film reels off the projector."

"That's a bit of a big deal. I mean, Johnny threaded the projectors . . . [schmuck]."

"Yeah. I know. Humor me, will ya?"

Pressing the intercom button, Dale, with just a tad bit of silent schmucky attitude, said:

"Hey, Johnny. Our DP here [schmuck] wants us to take the film off the projectors."

"Why the fuck would he . . . "

Dale took his hand off the intercom button, silencing the rest of the projectionist's query.

He went to help Johnny unthread the film.

Returning, Dale asked:

"Now what? [schmuck]"

"Now please give me your footlambert meter."

"You want the footlambert meter? [schmuck]"

"Yes please."

"Normally no one is allowed . . . "

"You know what? I'm sure that's the rule, Dale. But I flew all the way from New York, so how about you make an exception and please just give me the meter."

[Perhaps a silent schmuck from me to Dale.]

Dale went to the projection booth and came back with the Minolta 1° Spot meter.

"Here ya go," Dale said, silent schmucking the meter into my hand.

"Turn on projector one, please."

I took a reading.

"Now projector two."

I took a reading.

"Just checking. One more time. You say you, yourself read both these projectors this morning and you were getting 16 footlamberts from each one."

"Absolutely."

"You're sure about that?"

After a too long beat where Dale was doing some slow-motion internal calculations—what does Barry know that Dale doesn't?—backtracking, he said:

"Actually, Johnny took the readings."

"Not you?" I wondered.

"I thought your 'you' meant Deluxe. Not a specific person. [schmuck]"

"You want to check with Johnny one more time?" I asked, giving Dale an out.

"No need. Johnny checked. It's his job. And he said 16."

At this point, I'm flummoxed. Obviously, Dale knew I had some secret information that might contradict Johnny. Information that was going to make someone look really stupid. Yet Dale would not back down. I guess he was trained at the Bud Stone Deluxe-Don't-Give-a-Shit School.

"Let's get Bud Stone on the phone."

"Oh come on. What's the problem? [schmuck]"

"Here," I said, handing him the meter. "Read the screens."

"Give me a fuckin' break," he fake mumbled under his breath loud enough for me to hear.

We darkened the room, the screens were read, and the lights came back up.

"Yup," Dale admitted. "I see the problem. And I am very sorry," said the man who discovered he was color timing our print with projectors putting out 3, not 16, footlamberts. Timing our print with a very dim projector is why the film looked so bright at DuArt, an actual professional lab whose projectors are set to 16 footlamberts. Dale had to make the print incredibly bright, since there was so little light coming from his projectors.

Dale and I became friends. He was like a monkey in *The Wizard of Oz* that suddenly was freed from the tyranny of the Wicked

Witch. I would discover Dale was actually a good guy, and good color timer, but was suffering with a serious bout of DSS—Deluxe Stockholm Syndrome.

Over the years, Bud Stone's Deluxe Film Labs never got better. For the next 30 years I suffered. Over the last decade, as the method of recording and processing images changed from chemical [film] to electronic [digital] Deluxe, which closed its chemical lab in 2014, changing its name to Efilm, has taken this massive shift in stride and remains as horrible as it ever was. Dale left and started YCM, a business that was everything Deluxe wasn't. It was dedicated to preserving the beauty of film.

I'm not proud of this, but when Bud retired, replaced by a lovely man, Cyril Drabinsky, an Orthodox Jew who unfortunately wasn't able to break through the dreary, lazy Deluxe culture that Bud had created, I threatened to kidnap him on Yom Kippur, tie him to the roof of my car, and drive us to Deluxe where I was going to eat a pork and lobster sandwich while burning down his factory.

These were the years when I let my rage and anger have free rein over my mouth.

Which meant I didn't have sciatica.

When Barry Met Rob

In June 1988, with *Big* recently released, I was starting to get offers for my next job. This particular weekend two of Sweetie's single friends were hanging out at her house in East Hampton. One was Michele Singer, a dark-haired beauty who looked like an Israeli spy. She was a photographer, quick witted and brash. Leslie Simitch, her other guest, was equally sharp and forthcoming with opinions.

Two scripts had come in for weekend reading: *Men Don't Leave*, written and to be directed by Paul Brickman, his first movie since *Risky Business* and *When Harry Met Sally*, directed by Rob Reiner. I had worked with Rob when he had a one-day cameo on *Throw Momma from the Train*, and I liked him.

Sweetie, Leslie, Michele, and I spent part of the weekend reading the two scripts. Leslie and I chose *When Harry Met Sally*, a smart comedy that took place predominantly in New York, which was very appealing to me. Sweetie and Michele picked *Men Don't Leave*, a moving dramatic comedy that was going to film in Baltimore.

There are three bullet points that influence what movie I choose: money, location, and script. I'm not the only one in show biz using this same powerpoint presentation. Having come off *Big*, shot in New York, I was spoiled. I loved my New York film crew and back-to-back films where I could spend weekends at home in the Hamptons near Sweetie was a big plus.

Rob had directed some of my favorite movies and I also liked the themes of *When Harry Met Sally*.

Both scripts were very good. I could see why Sweetie and Michele picked *Men Don't Leave*. Many months later I shot some additional scenes for the film.

I chose *When Harry Met Sally* and met Rob for breakfast at the Carlyle Hotel. Also attending was Jane Musky, who Rob had already hired as the production designer. Jane and I had worked together on *Blood Simple* and *Raising Arizona*. Rob and I hit it off and I was hired.

Preproduction and some interiors were going to be photographed in Los Angeles, at which point we'd head to New York to film autumn foliage as well as some iconographic exteriors and remaining interiors.

On the first day of preproduction in LA, there was a *Premiere* magazine sitting on my desk. Michelle Pfeiffer was on the cover.

Looking down at the periodical, Rob said: "Hey, Ba. I'm thinking about asking Michelle out on a date. What do ya think?"

"Well, you can date her if you want, but once we get to New York I'm introducing you to another Michele—Michele Singer—and you're going to marry her."

Before we got to New York we filmed a specific scene I'm proud of. The script called for a triptych split screen phone conversation. Billy Crystal on the left side of the frame, Meg Ryan on the right, and in the middle Carrie Fisher and Bruno Kirby in bed together. This scene went on for multiple pages and the challenge was that every actor had to get every line of the multi-paged scene right or the take was ruined. The lines also required four actors perfectly landing their comic timing. Rob didn't want to cheat by cutting to a close-up to combine takes. He wanted the entire several-minute scene to play out as one continuous shot.

This is how it was accomplished:

We built three sets on one sound stage.

Billy, Meg, and Bruno and Carrie each had their own one wall set, separated by a great distance so their voices didn't contaminate the other actors' dialogue. All the performers could hear each other through their phones. Rob had a big monitor set up with a split screen of all three sets so he could see his final shot in progress. It took 76 takes, since if any actor messed up even a word, right up to the end of the take, we'd have to cut and start over. The tension would increase the closer we got to the end of the scene: Please don't fuck up, please don't fuck up, please don't . . . Damn. But at the end of the day, we left the set knowing we had a perfect take.

The stage we used was Stage 3/8 at Hollywood Center Studios. It used to be two stages—3 *and* 8, which were combined for the Las Vegas street scenes in Francis Ford Coppola's *One from the Heart*. At the time, Francis owned the entire studio lot so he could make this happen. The strange thing about Stage 3/8 is I shot part or all of *Throw Momma from the Train*, *When Harry Met Sally*, *Misery*, and directed *The Addams Family* on this one stage. In fact, these movies were the first four films I worked on in Los Angeles. At some point I said to Sweetie,

"Given how LA is considered the film capital of the world, you'd think they'd have more than one stage."

After a few weeks of filming in LA, we moved production to New York, and it was bliss. I loved the film crew, it was autumn, the most perfect time to be in New York and the locations were beautiful. I was hanging out with Sweetie on weekends in East Hampton, or when she came into the city. I also loved working with Rob.

One challenge was everyone in Manhattan recognized him, and the only time people weren't ruining sound takes shouting "Meathead"—the nickname of Rob's character on *All in the*

Family—was when we were in Spanish Harlem, where the chant of "Carne Cabeza" would ring out—also ruining takes.

Now that we were in New York, Sweetie brought Michele Singer around to have lunch [as far as I know, Rob never asked Michelle Pfeiffer out on a date]. Because we were filming in Manhattan, instead of a catered lunch, the crew broke for an hour plus "walking time," so we always had about an hour and fifteen minutes to eat. Lunch was with Rob, Michele, Sweetie, Billy Crystal, Nora Ephron, and me. Sweetie and I didn't think it went well. For one thing, Michele vaguely suggested to Nora she might be anorexic.

After lunch Rob and I walked back to the set.

"She's a tad arch," he offered.

"Uh, yeah."

"Could you ask if I could get her phone number?"

That weekend, Sweetie and I double dated with Rob and Michele at Amsterdam, an Upper West Side restaurant.

As Michele lit up a cigarette [this was the '80s and you could do such a thing], Rob inquired, "Why do you smoke so much?"

Michele replied, "Why are you so fat?"

Sweetie and I were pretty sure I'd be fired later that night.

The two of them started to date and several years later came to Sweetie's and my wedding in New Orleans, which combined our nuptials with the *Miller's Crossing* wrap party.

A month after our wedding, Rob and Michele were married in Hawaii.

Make It About Them

As much as Rob and I enjoyed working together, that's how little Nora Ephron liked me. I think she was annoyed I didn't take myself as seriously as she viewed herself. Late in the New York schedule we were on a small set built for rain cover. The location was Sally's bedroom. Harry and Sally just had sex, and Billy is staring at the digital alarm clock waiting for morning so he can leave.

Lighting Polaroid. Camera matte box in foreground.

As we were lining up an insert of Billy's point of view of the clock on Meg's nightstand, I yelled,

"Hey Rob. Should we do a Dutch tilt so it looks like a shot from a Godard movie?"

I had never seen a Godard film.

Before Rob could respond, Nora, sitting next to him yelled, "Can you save us all the fucking film school bullshit!"

"It's a joke, Nora."

I enjoyed working with all the actors. Billy and I joked around a lot, and Carrie Fisher shared she had a crush on me though she admitted she knew nothing could come between Sweetie and me.

I learned an important lesson on that movie, which was if you want help from an actor or director make it about *them*. We were filming a massively long walk and talk at night in SoHo. I didn't like using a Steadicam—a camera with gyroscopes attached to the waist of the camera operator—and instead laid several hundred feet of dolly track—a multi-hour undertaking.

When filming a night scene, you want a strong backlight. The best way to achieve that is to put a series of lights in the bucket of a man lift or crane, raise it high enough so the lights are out of frame, and aim them in various directions. I used both Mole Richardson 10K fresnels and Maxi Brutes that had nine 1,000 watt bulbs. In New York we rented cranes from Blakley Tree Service. Blakley had a specific vehicle that was, believe it or not, a 210-foot crane. That's the height of a 21-story building. It articulated at 150 feet allowing us to hide the crane around the corner of a building, send the lights straight up the full 150 feet, then articulate the remaining 60 feet at a 90-degree angle. Now the lights are floating 150 feet in the air and out of frame over the middle of a New York street. It was an impressive undertaking.

We rehearsed this very long dialogue scene with Billy, Bruno, Carrie, and Meg. They walked along West Broadway as they read the lines from their sides [5x7-inch xeroxes of the script pages]. The actors then went into hair and makeup while the crew lit the scene. The problem is that actors, with few exceptions [Albert Finney, Gene Hackman, Tommy Lee Jones], usually don't come to set having memorized all their lines. They kind of know them but usually learn the exact words during their on-set rehearsal and in the hair and makeup trailer.

Our four actors have now come back to the set having memorized their lines. This means they are no longer looking at their sides as they slowly walk and talk, and are now walking faster since they're looking straight ahead. Unfortunately, they end up an additional 50 feet beyond where we're lit and where we've laid dolly track.

"Hey Rob: Can you ask the actors to slow down? They're moving much faster than they did during rehearsal and they're *way* beyond the mark we're lit for."

"I don't want them worrying about anything but acting, Ba. Can you light it so they can stop wherever they want?"

"Sure. Give me fourteen minutes."

I never gave estimates in round numbers. More specific numbers, like 14, or 11, or 17, made it seem like I really gave it some thought.

There are two kinds of cinematographers: Those that light a location, with general illumination where the actors can stand vaguely where you planned and still be lit. This method tends to be flatter and less theatrical. The other kind of director of photography, and I was in this camp, lights each shot individually. This lighting tends to be more flattering but more demanding of the actors since they have to be on a specific mark.

What Rob had asked me to do, by saying he wanted the actors to stop anywhere, was to flatten the lighting and make it more general, which I did. While the grips added more track, I added another 75 feet of soft ambient lighting so even if the actors picked up their pace, they'd still have an exposure.

"Ready, Rob."

"Will it still be pretty Ba? Will it still look beautiful?"

"It won't look *as* pretty, but it won't look terrible, and the actors can stop wherever they want."

"We don't want '*not terrible*.' We want pretty. Where do they have to stop for the shot to be beautiful?"

I walked Rob back to the original marks, where the actors had stopped during rehearsals.

"Hey guys," Rob said, as he had the four actors come back to the original marks. "Slow your walk down and stop here."

I turned off the new lights and the scene looked great. Plus, I had just learned an important lesson.

We now had to light for Meg's close-up.

For the first few weeks, although Meg was great fun to work with, it was still early in her career and she was rarely able to accommodate my needs in terms of lighting. Try as I might, asking her to stop on a certain mark, or to lean on a left or right foot to keep her shadow off another actor, was always hit or miss. This night, I tried a new approach. Instead of asking Meg to hit a certain mark, I changed my request to make it not about my needs, but hers:

"Hey Meg. It doesn't matter where you stop, but if you land right here on this mark, you look fantastic."

It worked so well it became my new approach, not only with Meg, but all future actors. I let it be Meg's choice whether she wanted to look her best.

She hit her mark every time.

I'll Have What She's Having

One of the most iconic scenes in the history of movie comedies takes place at Katz's Deli, where Meg Ryan fakes an orgasm. It was a difficult day of shooting. The scene was quite long and we had only one day to film it. The deli had the humidity of a Russian bath, since all their brisket, corned beef, and pastrami are kept moist in steam trays. It was a warm day, we had no auxiliary air-conditioning, had a lot of hot lights inside the restaurant to balance the interior to the exterior exposure, and Rob was under a lot of stress. He was directing a young actress to fake an orgasm while in the presence of a room full of extras, including Estelle Reiner, his mother.

Estelle gives the famous:

"I'll have what she's having," zinger at the end of the scene.

It was so hot in the room, Rob asked a meat carver for a spare towel, which he wore on his head to absorb his sweat, with the added benefit of him smelling deliciously like pastrami.

It was a bad day for me as well, since I had just learned Sweetie's husband, Elliott, had missed another divorce court appearance due to a "last-minute" job in France. The next available court date was eight months in the future.

A really bad day.

The scene, however, was historic and I learned an essential rule of comedy:

It's all about the reaction shot.

I watched the scene in various recruited audience screenings while Rob was cutting the film. Each time it played, as huge as the laughter was for Meg faking her orgasm, the laugh level jumped exponentially when Rob cut to Billy's reaction shot. The reaction shot is the audience's point of view. It will always get the biggest laugh.

Lighting Polaroid. Katz's Deli. Estelle Reiner in the background.

Men in Hats

In early fall of 1988, one night ahead of Hurricane Florence, the Coen Brothers and I moved into the CANAL PLACE Hotel in New Orleans, where we would spend the next six months working on *Miller's Crossing*. Joel and Ethan weren't great drivers, I was a lousy navigator, and this was years before Google Maps, but we could always find our way back home by heading towards the rooftop sign that spelled our hotel's name in huge red neon letters.

Although only a Category 1, Florence managed to destroy one of the letters of our hotel's name. The hotelier neither fixed nor turned off the rest of the sign during our time in residence.

For the next eight months, whenever I'd ask the brothers where they wanted to have dinner, Ethan would reply: "The ANAL PLACE."

Sweetie and I were in our rental car, following Joel and Ethan in theirs, as we drove towards Lake Pontchartrain to scout locations. It was 1989 and I was the only one who owned a cell phone. It rang.

"Are you anywhere near the boys?" asked John Lyons, one of our casting directors. "It's a bit of an emergency."

I flashed my headlights, both cars pulled over and Joel walked back towards my car. I handed him the phone:

"Jesus. Yeah, OK. Well, let me know when it happens."

The part of Leo the mob boss was written for Trey Williams, who played Nathan Arizona, the father of quintuplets, in *Raising Arizona*. John was calling Joel to report the shocking news that

Trey had suffered a brain aneurism and would not live. With only two weeks before the start of principal photography, we needed a new co-star.

Albert Finney arrived a week before we started filming. Being a British actor, he was always prepared, knowing every word of dialogue for each day's scene—quite impressive since each night he, along with several of our electricians, closed down the New Orleans' bars.

Albert loved working on the film so much he asked Joel and Ethan if he could be in one more scene. Joel told him the next day was the last day of photography and it took place in the women's lounge at the club—the only male in the scene being Gabriel Byrne.

"Make me the female washroom attendant."

Albert as the matron bathroom attendant.

As we did before filming *Blood Simple* and *Raising Arizona*, Joel, Ethan, and I screened *Dr. Strangelove* and *The Conformist*. We watched

Strangelove because we loved it, and *The Conformist* because we were thrilled by how stylized it was, from camera angles to wardrobe to lighting. We also stole from it—both *Miller's Crossing* and *The Conformist* climax with a scene in the woods and both have a killer blow on his hands to warm them before unzipping their pants to urinate.

I wanted to duplicate the soft muted dreariness of *The Conformist's* woods and told the Coens we could only film the forest scenes on overcast days.

"Good luck with that," the Coens laughed.

Except for one shot, I pulled it off.

Although most of the film was shot with Kodak's fine grain 5247 film stock, Kodak's color palette tends towards a bright, saturated, emerald green. Perfect for the children's pop-up book style of *Raising Arizona* but totally wrong for *Miller's Crossing's* forests. All the scenes in the woods were shot on Fujifilm, a much softer, lower contrast look with the added advantage of its green leaning towards teal.

The boys called *Miller's Crossing* "Men in Hats." We introduced the hat motif in the opening credit sequence where a fedora falls into frame, sits there for a second, then picked up by the wind, floats high and away from the lens. If we were filming in 2024, we'd shoot the background and have a computer graphics' hat do the heavy lifting. But this was 1988 and a computer-generated hat for a shot like this would have cost many tens of thousands of dollars.

Our challenges were:

1. Throwing the hat so it landed exactly in the middle of the frame.
2. Not seeing the monofilament that was tied to the back of the fedora, which pulled it up and away towards the distant trees.

3. Getting the hat to flip and rise, as opposed to sledding along the ground. Even when we managed [one in eight tries] to get the hat tossed into the center of the frame, we were having trouble pulling the hat so it lofted into the air. It scooted away from the camera as if a crab.

Peter Chesney, our physical effects person, who I would scream at seven years later on *Men in Black* [more about that later], needed something that would be invisible to the camera but force the hat to flip once it started to be pulled by the monofilament. If we could flip the hat, the aerodynamics of the shape would make it fly instead of skate along the ground. Look closely, and you'll see three sticks in the ground behind the hat.

The hat being pulled into the distance, flipping thanks to those three sticks.

We managed to get the shot seconds before the sun appeared over the morning gloom.

John Turturro, who played Bernie Bernbaum, the needy gay villain, approached me at the wrap party [also known as Sweetie's and my wedding]:

"Hey Ba. Thank you so much."

"You're welcome, John, but why the thanks?"

"My entire performance was based on mimicking you."

"*Really?*" [not a silent schmuck]

"Well, not the gay stuff. But Bernie's whining and neediness? That's all you, Ba."

Crawl to the Loogie

Misery was my last film as a cinematographer. A few things went wrong that first day on the set. We were somewhere in the Reno / Lake Tahoe area shooting what would be the first scene of the film. Writer Paul Sheldon, played by Jimmy Caan, having finished typing the last line of his latest novel, is scripted to pop open a bottle of champagne, ignite a strike anywhere kitchen match with his thumb, and light the one cigarette he allows himself upon completing a new novel.

Jimmy was, let's just say . . . energetic. He was in many ways the worst actor to put in bed for more than half a movie. The man could not sit still. He was highly strung and seemed to have ADHD.

The morning started off badly when I mistakenly ordered biscuits and gravy from the catering truck. I'm more of a burnt bacon, two runny egg yolk eggs and cheese on a buttered kaiser roll, or a breakfast burrito with scrambled egg, cheese, potato, avocado, salsa, hot sauce, and burnt bacon kind of guy, but this morning, the start of a new film, I thought I'd branch out.

Cut to ten minutes later and me vomiting my biscuits and gravy behind a tree.

I recovered and walked over to the set, a small cabin surrounded by snow. Director Rob Reiner, the script supervisor, first assistant director, prop guy, and I rehearsed with Jimmy. It was an easy scene [we thought] to start our show: Finish typing, pull out the last sheet of paper from the typewriter, open a bottle of Dom Pérignon, and light a strike anywhere match with your thumb, an easy thing to pull off made even easier by a small piece of flint we had discretely taped to the off-camera part of Jimmy's thumb.

No dialogue.

One actor.

A couple of props.

Rob made a few adjustments, we showed a rehearsal to the key members of the crew [grip, sound, electric, camera, stand-in], at which point Jimmy went to hair and makeup and I lit the set.

There may have been six camera setups for the entire scene: wide shot to show the interior of the cabin, a medium shot of Jimmy and his typewriter, an extreme close-up of "The End" being typed, an insert of the last page of his book being added to the rest of his finished manuscript, popping the champagne cork, and a medium shot of him lighting his cigarette. This should have taken four hours, at most. Jimmy could not stop fidgeting, could not stop swaying back and forth like an extremely enthusiastic rabbi davening during Yom Kippur, and could not get the strike anywhere match to strike anywhere. At six hours into filming, we called lunch. We hadn't finished the scene. I joined Rob in his camper which now included his new bride, Michele.

Despite the snow outside, Rob was sweating profusely. I mean this was day one; Jimmy couldn't stand still without undulating like an air dancer at a used car dealership, and his character was about to spend *a lot* of time confined to a bed.

"Hey Rob. Remember Vietnam?" I said.

Rob and Michele got the reference and started to laugh.

"No. No. Seriously. Get out now. Get out before it's too late. You don't want to lose tens of thousands of metaphorical troops and then have to say, 'We can't leave now. We've lost too many precious young men.' Or in this case, 'We can't fire him now, we're four weeks into shooting.'"

"I can't do that, Ba. We're ready to go. We built sets, have a crew ..."

"And that's exactly what Lyndon Johnson said for six years. Get out now, Rob."

I only half meant it, and obviously we couldn't fire Jimmy on day one, but it was tough going for the 12 weeks of photography, especially the 9 filmed in one room.

After a few days on location, we traveled to Los Angeles where almost all of the filming took place on the only stage I had ever worked on—Stage 3/8 at Hollywood Center Studios.

When Rob and I first talked about doing *Misery* he was considering Bette Midler for the female lead opposite Caan. Although lovely [I directed her five years later in *Get Shorty*], I thought a better idea would be Kathy Bates. I had seen her on Broadway in *Night Mother* and she was amazing. I also knew her a tad since she was friends with Joel and Ethan.

Bette passed on Rob's offer, and Rob met and hired Kathy.

Kathy and I enjoyed working together.

Each morning she would greet me with a:

"Fuck you, Sonnenfeld."

And I would reply with a happy:

"Fuck you, Bates."

She had a brilliant and unusual way of acting that was full of technical proficiency and self-confidence. Most actors despise line readings—a director acting out how they want a sentence or phrase to be spoken. An actor feels that it's their job to decide how a line is said. They don't want to imitate someone else's delivery.

When Rob approached Kathy after a take and would start to remind her that she was socially awkward, rarely spoke to others, lived alone ... Kathy would say,

"Give me a line reading, Rob."

Rob would act out exactly how he wanted the line spoken. This saved a lot of discussion and extra takes because Kathy now knew what Rob wanted. "I get it. He wants me angrier—or really wants me to hit a certain word." She had enough self-confidence to make it her own and give a brilliant performance.

When Kathy won her Golden Globe Award, in addition to Rob, she thanked me in her acceptance speech. Unfortunately, one of the actresses she had competed against was Anjelica Huston, nominated for her role in *The Grifters*. I was presently directing Anjelica in *The Addams Family*.

The next day Anjelica, who was usually a couple of hours in hair and makeup, took almost five. I called Kathy the day before the Academy Awards and suggested if she won the Oscar—Kathy was once again competing against Anjelica— not to thank me. She did and didn't. Anjelica came out of hair and makeup in her usual two hours.

I was busy filming *Miller's Crossing*, the last movie I photographed for the Coens, and was not involved in the set design for *Misery*. The production designer, Norman Garwood, oversaw construction of Kathy Bates' house, built entirely on stage. Norman had designed *Brazil*, a brilliant looking movie, and had worked with Rob on his wonderful *The Princess Bride*. Like most, but not all, production designers [Bo Welch and Michael Wylie being exceptions] there is sometimes an uncomfortable relationship between production designer and cinematographer. There's often jealousy and a competition for the director's attention. In Norman's case, he designed and built the main set without consulting me.

On *Throw Momma from the Train*, Ida Random, the film noir–named production designer, was outraged when I asked her to paint a set a certain color—in fact it was the set that Rob Reiner acted in.

"Hey Ida. Can you paint that office we're filming on location with Danny and Rob this color green," I said as I showed her a color swatch from my Pantone book. "We have a large page count that day and I won't have time to flag the light off the walls. If the walls are green, the actors' faces will separate from the background, color-wise, and I can work a lot faster."

"I've worked with Vilmos Zsigmond and László Kovács and they *never* told me what color to paint a wall!"

"I know, Ida. But they're really good. Way better than me. I need your help much more than they did."

Ida painted the set green.

Because Norman didn't coordinate with me, he built the interior of Kathy Bates' two-story house with the second floor on top of the first. This meant the first floor was structurally holding up the set above. I couldn't move any walls to get certain shots since the second floor was supported by the first. I also couldn't hang lights above the bedroom set, using a grid of pipes hung from the stage's roof, since there was a hard ceiling and an entire second floor sitting above the bedroom. This was a disaster since most of the script took place in the first floor's bedroom.

After a week and a half of filming on stage, a worried Rob came to me:

"Hey Ba. We're two days behind schedule and we're just getting started."

"I know Rob. I hate to tell you this, but the second floor should have been built on the stage floor and not right above us. We never connect the two floors in a shot, and there was no reason to build it like this. The only way we're going to make up those two days, and not fall at least a day behind every week is to remove that second floor and rebuild it on the ground. Then I can start lighting from above and start pulling some walls when we need to get further back. We're dying here, as you know."

"But . . ."

"Yeah, I know it will be expensive but I checked with the crew and they can move the set over the three-day weekend and I promise we'll make up the time and money, and even finish ahead of schedule."

Rob agreed to the solution and we caught up to our original schedule.

Jimmy Caan and I had a good time together but man, he could not sit still. The guy was wired. He was a series of contradictions. A Jew—and rodeo star. He must have fallen off his horse a lot, since his back looked like a spatchcocked chicken if cut up by a blind chef on a roller coaster. He was a tough guy—yet extremely sensitive. One day between setups I asked Jimmy if it was true he used to live at the Playboy Mansion.

"You know, Ba. That was a good run. Not only did I live there, I had sex with the Playmate of the Month for sixteen straight months."

"What was the month that refused ya, Jimmy?"

"You know I can't tell ya that."

"I'm not asking for a name. Just a month. Was she a Miss July? Or a November?"

"Can't tell ya, Ba. I'm discreet that way."

Jimmy could not just lie in that bed. He really was Rob's Vietnam. At some point Rob and I had run out of patience with his whining and fidgeting. I had set up a very low angle tracking shot where Jimmy rolls out of bed and slowly crawls towards his bedroom's door.

"Hey Ba," Jimmy yelled from the bed. "How far do you want me to crawl?"

This is truly horrible, but instead of putting down a colored piece of tape on the floor, called a "mark," which is what we'd normally do, I actually spat on the floor.

"Crawl to the loogie, Jimmy," Rob yelled to his star.

Misery's Misery

I always viewed my role of cinematographer as the "friend of the director," more than the director of photography. I had as many opinions and ideas about editing, performance, or if the costumes looked worn-in enough, as I did about lighting or camera angles. Whether it was with DeVito, Penny Marshall, Rob, or the Coens, I was often involved in areas that were more the purview of the director. I would truly hate me if I had to direct a movie with me as cinematographer.

Rob would often tell me I should direct, and I would tell him I had no interest, which was true. That all changed two weeks before the completion of *Misery* when producer Scott Rudin out of nowhere offered me *The Addams Family* to direct.

The Monday after my meeting with Rudin I came to work and at some point told Rob that I had been offered a directing job. That was a mistake. Now, instead of being the cinematographer, or "friend of the director," I was another director on the set and no one, unless they're brothers, wants that.

Rob doesn't enjoy filming stunts. He's very comfortable directing actors acting, but less so directing action scenes. The last shot we did before lunch, the day I told Rob I was going to be a director, was Jimmy Caan shoving burnt manuscript pages into Kathy's mouth while they wrestle on the floor, eventually rolling out of frame. As was anything with Jimmy, it was a challenge to get the specificity of action we needed. We finally got a good take, they rolled out of frame with great energy, and Rob called lunch.

The first shot back from our catered meal we set up a new camera angle to film Jimmy and Kathy, burnt papers in her mouth, rolling into frame and continuing their struggle. I finished lighting, we called in the cast, and we shot one take.

"Cut. Moving on," Rob announced, which meant he was happy with that one take and we were going to set up the camera for the next shot. As I say, Rob really doesn't like filming stunts, and Jimmy made it that much more difficult.

"Hey Rob."

"Yeah?"

"I think you might want to get another take. As a safety. One where . . . "

"It's fine, Barry. Moving on."

"I mean, we always do more than one take, and this is a big stunt, and there's nothing else to cut to."

"We're good."

Now I'm being annoying. The director has said three times he wants to move on and I'm still pushing. If I were the director, I would have fired me.

"It's just. In the shot before lunch, they rolled out of frame really quickly, and in this shot, they rolled into frame really slowly."

[The first shot after lunch actors never have the same energy because they've either taken a nap or are putting all their strength into digesting their tri-tip.]

I continued: "There's no other coverage for this part of the scene and I don't think it will cut together."

At this point, Rob has had enough.

Rob was angry and my head was throbbing. I knew how annoying I was being. Rob called the crew to the set.

This is what Rob said:

"Baaaaaary thinks I should go again.

"Baaaaaary thinks it won't cut together.

"But here's the thing: There is only one director on the set. And it isn't you [as he points to a random person], or you, or you or you or you. And it's not Baaaaary. It's me."

"Of course it's you, Rob. Of course it's you. Maybe I'm wrong, but I don't think it will cut together. Ask Todd."

Rob turned to Todd Henry, our excellent camera operator.

"Todd?!"

Todd was teetering on a tight wire. His immediate boss was me, and I'm a steady source of employment for him, but then again, there's Rob fucking Reiner asking him to choose sides.

"Why don't you look at playback?" Todd wisely advised.

Rob looked at the video of the shot before lunch where the actors energetically rolled out of frame, and the shot we just had a disagreement about where they lazily rolled into frame, and announced:

"Let's go again."

Rob and I did not speak to each other the last days of our shoot. Nor for several years after that.

If the situation was reversed, I would have been at least as angry as Rob. Directing is really hard. There is constant pressure and anxiety. Every fucking person thinks it's their job to help you, and sometimes all you want is to be left alone to make your own decision even if it's wrong. Hesitate on the set for more than two seconds and you'll hear suggestions. You are never given any time to just think.

Although the Kathy/Jimmy wrestling match was a specific situation, it kind of explains why I'm a neurotic for preproduction. If you make every possible decision before you get to the set [although no amount of prep could have helped this event], you'll reduce those silent seconds of *thinking*, and you won't have any annoying "friend of the director" making you question your decisions.

One of my favorite activities when working in Los Angeles is eating Chinese food. Chinois on Main, Wolfgang Puck's French-Asian fusion joint in Santa Monica, or Mr. Chow in Beverly Hills are excellent choices. The left side of Mr. Chow has six round tables that seem to always have directors sitting at them. Maybe we're all big maître d' tippers. Sweetie and I were in Los Angeles several years after Rob and I stopped talking. We had just finished our meal, which included shrimp dumplings, gambler's duck, filet mignon, drunken fish, green shrimp, some lychee nuts for dessert, and martinis—Tanqueray gin for Sweetie, brutally shaken Belvedere vodka with no vermouth for me. We were at one of those six round tables—in fact the table Mr. Chow historically held for Billy Wilder at the front of the restaurant.

Standing up to leave I saw Rob and Michele farther down the row of directors' tables.

Sweetie doesn't like confrontation. I'm OK with it—I'm the member of our duo who gets the assignment of firing people.

"Let's say hi."

"Please don't," said Sweetie.

"We love them, we miss them, and it's going to be fine."

"What if it isn't?"

"We're not going to have a fight in Mr. Chow. I'm going over."

Sweetie hung back at our table.

Rob and Michele were in conversation and didn't see me walk up.

"Hey guys. What's new?"

"Ba. How are ya? Is Sweetie here?"

I waved her over.

And just like that we were once again friends. It has been over 30 years since we made up and not only are we still very close, Rob has optioned my memoir, *Barry Sonnenfeld, Call Your Mother,* to see if we can make it into a movie.

Not a Manly Man

Directing The Addams Family.

Scott Rudin was the president of production at 20th Century Fox when I shot both *Raising Arizona* and *Big* for his studio. He had since become an independent producer and was looking for a director for *The Addams Family*. He wanted a visually stylized comedy and, as he told me after both Terry Gilliam and Tim Burton passed:

"Since I can't get any good directors, I decided to take a chance on you."

Rudin is a persuasive gent and convinced Orion Pictures to hire me.

Most big budget movies complete from twelve to twenty camera setups a day. Owen Roizman, *The Addams Family* cinematographer, was a brilliant cameraman but profoundly slow. The camera setup that caused me to faint took most of a day to light.

Thing, the disembodied hand, hearing a knock at the Addams' door, sits up out of his slumber, cracks his knuckles a couple of times, and races from the séance room through several hallways, rooms, and antechambers to the front door. In painful retrospect, this shot should have been filmed by the second unit camera crew since it had no principal actors except Christopher Hart's hand. We were using an extremely wide lens, the camera was very low to the ground, and we were dollying the camera following Thing through many rooms. There were few places to hide lights and I had broken my promise to Owen that I'd never make him pan. Still, ten hours to light this one shot was perverse.

Let's chat about Thing. In Charles Addams' cartoons, Thing is never revealed and is referred to as something so hideous that it should not be seen. In the TV series, Thing became a disembodied hand inside a box. It was played by the same actor who played Lurch, which was nuts since the guy was six feet nine inches tall and took up a lot of acreage.

I wanted our Thing to be mobile, allowing me to track with him as he moved from room to room. Since my whole raison d'être is putting a wide angle lens close to the ground and racing the camera through space, Thing was my perfect character. But how do I cast for Thing? I thought hiring a magician would be smart, since I could have Thing do magic tricks like rolling a quarter across his knuckles or doing one handed card tricks.

A casting breakdown was sent out from our casting director, David Rubin. A week later I was sitting in a room with David and his assistant, Debbie Zane [who became a major casting director in her own right], asking a hundred magicians, over the course of an entire day, to walk their hand across a table and roll a quarter across their knuckles.

"Now show me fear."

"Now joy."

"Excitement!" [How a hand is supposed to delineate excitement from joy is a tough one.]

"Now Thing is sad."

"Bored."

I hated myself.

The problem, as it turns out, is that most magicians who are well versed in sleight of hand almost by definition move their hands in jerky, not fluid motions in order to disguise their trickery. At the end of the day, we were nowhere.

"I never thought I would say this, and I know I'll regret it, but call in the mimes."

"Really?" Debbie silently schmucked me.

"Thing is an important member of the family and could be comedy gold if we can find the right hand. But any mime who comes into the room walking against the wind, kick him out."

As I suspected, the mimes made me extremely uncomfortable. Back to magicians.

Luckily Chris Hart, a fine magician, showed up. He had great looking hands, long fingers, and could move his hand in a graceful way. Chris was hired and indeed was comedy gold. His Morse code discussion with Raul at the end of the movie was first rate acting.

Arriving home after Owen's ten hours of lighting, I was deeply depressed. We had fallen yet another day behind schedule and there were rumors of Orion's pending bankruptcy. I also realized, driving back to the apartment, I had filmed the shot incorrectly: I had no way to cut out of it. I needed a cutaway to bridge the shot of

Thing running to the front door, and the door opening. How could I have sat around for ten hours and not realized I needed a way to get out of that long tracking shot before the door opened?

I stayed awake all night pondering my few options—one that I could give to the second unit crew, since the last thing I needed was for first unit to fall further behind schedule. I trusted our second unit cameraman, Bill Pope, a fellow classmate from film school, who later went on to shoot the first three Matrix movies, the second and third Spider-Man movies, and years later, *Men in Black 3* for me. I knew he could match Owen's lighting at a much faster clip.

At 5:30 AM, which was when I needed to shower and dress for my drive to the set, I finally devised two additional shots: a side angle push-in of Thing entering frame, crashing into the door, then leaping up and out of frame; and from there, I'd cut to another second unit shot of the door handle. Thing would enter frame from below, pull down on the handle, and open the door. Unfortunately, it took the entire night to figure out this solution, which meant I was heading to the set without having slept.

We were weeks into filming, falling further behind schedule. I saw no end to my nightmare.

It's the next morning and I'm standing at the bottom of the stairs in the Richard Macdonald designed entryway waiting for Owen to finish lighting. I've just downed my fifth espresso in hopes of compensating for my waking night of hell, when suddenly, an invisible giant balloon blows up inside my chest. The room goes out of focus, then irises down to dark brown, then black. Owen yells, "Someone get a blanket" as I collapse to the floor.

I vaguely remember being rolled onto a sound blanket—otherwise known as a furniture pad. With a crew member on each corner, I was hammocked off the set and across the lot where I had a tiny office. I woke up on the couch, with Rudin and a nurse staring down at me as if I had died.

"What happened?" I groggily asked.

"He lives!" bellowed Rudin, in his version of sympathy.

"Is Owen done lighting?"

"Done lighting?! We shut down for the day. You're going home."

"Scott, we can't do that. We're too behind schedule. I'm fine. Get the crew back."

"Don't be ridiculous. You're going home and getting some rest."

I started to cry.

"This is so unmanly."

"Let's face it," said Rudin:

"You're not a manly man."

A few hours after I was dropped off at my rental apartment at the Sea Colony in Santa Monica, a package arrived. It was from Scott, David Rubin, and Marc Shaiman, the movie's composer, all gay men. In it was a Chippendales photo calendar, a Barbra Streisand record album, and a photo of Judy Garland. The card read, "Welcome to the world of Dorothy."

The Key Light Clause

Anjelica Huston's agent was calling.

"Baaaary. It's Toni Howard. Listen, Anjelica needs a key light clause."

"A key light clause?"

"Anjelica is taking a chance with you as a first time director, and she needs to know she'll have a key light clause."

"Well, sure, Toni. It's just that a key . . . "

"She needs it in her contract, Barry. And Paramount won't give it to her. And unless she gets it, she's not doing your movie."

Although I hadn't yet met Toni in person, I already liked her—she was feisty and direct.

"A key light is just the brightest light in a shot, Toni. That's the actual definition of a 'key light.' Anjelica doesn't want to worry about a 'key light' since every shot has a 'brightest light.' What she wants is to be lit beautifully. And truthfully, you can't really put that in a contract, can you?"

"She's worried, Barry."

"Tell Anjelica I know my way around lighting and I promise she'll always be beautifully lit. I will protect her. How's that?"

"Thank you. And good luck."

I talked to Owen about giving Morticia, Anjelica's character, her own motivated lighting no matter where she was in a room, or what light source she was near. She should be photographed as if lit by George Hurrell, the famous Hollywood glamour photographer.

Owen did a fantastic job making Anjelica look beautiful. Roizman was a cranky guy, once making Anjelica cry when he told her makeup woman, in front of Anjelica, "I'm a cameraman, not a surgeon."

After ten weeks, Owen left the film for a previous commitment to be replaced by a less talented, but less cranky Gale Tattersall. Anjelica thought she liked Gale more than Owen, since he was a nice man with a British accent, until she saw the finished film and realized what an extraordinary job Owen had done during his time on *The Addams Family*. We had yet another DP for a few days when Gale came down with a serious sinus infection. I moved my buddy Bill Pope up from second unit DP to first unit for the few days Gale was out sick.

The scene Pope shot took place in the school auditorium where Pugsley and Wednesday were performing in their school play—a sword fight with a very "Addams Family" ending.

Bill lit the school's lobby where we were starting our day's work. I could tell Anjelica was in a bad mood. She wouldn't look where I needed, and I knew why.

A decade earlier, when Bill and I were film school classmates, Sydney Pollack came to NYU to preview his new movie, *Three Days of the Condor*. One of the funny stories he told was Cliff Robertson's refusal to look where Sydney needed for a shot. Try as he might, Sydney could not get Cliff to hold his look. Ironically the cinematographer on the film, Owen Roizman, called Sydney aside:

"I know the problem. Give me ten minutes." [I came to learn firsthand that Owen's "ten minutes" was an hour forty.]

Sydney continued with his story:

"Owen brought the biggest light he had on the truck, a Mole Richardson 10K, and put it exactly where I needed Cliff to look. He put so many double nets in the fixture that there was virtually no light reaching Cliff on the set, but Cliff saw that big Mole Richardson and looked right at it, every take.

"Cliff was looking for his key light," said Sidney.

I took Pope aside:

"Get a 10K off the truck, put a bunch of double nets in it so it doesn't change the exposure and put it right over the top of the camera. Fuss over Anjelica, take a lot of light readings, move the light up an inch, back down, then up again, give the OK signal to the gaffer, and we'll be fine. She's looking for her key light."

Owen Roizman and Anjelica Huston. Owen sets her "key light."

Grazer vs. the Coens

The Addams Family was a box office success and I was a "hot" director, but I was broke. First time directors get paid Directors Guild of America minimum scale, which meant the year and a half it took to make the film I earned about a quarter of what I would have made as a cinematographer. *The Addams Family* was released Thanksgiving 1991. The film cost $30 million and eventually grossed $192 million at the worldwide box office, although Paramount's profit and loss statement showed the picture was a hundred million in the red.

"Grow up and sue us like everybody else," said Paramount chairwoman Sherry Lansing, when asked about the discrepancy.

Brian Grazer, who co-owned Imagine Films with Ron Howard, offered me *The Concierge*, later changed to *For Love or Money* since Universal Pictures didn't think most Americans knew what a concierge was. The film starred Michael J. Fox. Although the script needed work [almost all of them do], it felt vaguely *Breakfast at Tiffany's*-ish. In addition, the movie checked most of the boxes on my how to choose a movie powerpoint:

Location: New York and the Hamptons. Check.
Money: More than I've ever earned, and desperately needed. Check.
Script: Needs a rewrite but could get better. Half a check.

Sold!

The Coen Brothers had yet to get into the rewrite business, but as a big favor to me agreed to do some rewriting on the script.

Brian Grazer is a bit of a "character." He has very little body fat, almost always wears a skinny tie, and has spiked hair. I applaud his schtick. Any affectation that gets you remembered is the way to go in my book. Starting out as a cinematographer, I always wore a tie; whenever a producer was thinking about hiring an inexpensive cameraman to film some second unit shots for their non-union movie, they'd say: "The skinny kid with the tie was a hard worker, let's hire him." I still wear a tie on set. Recently I was at a luncheon for Marty Scorsese, who had just screened his latest film, *Killers of the Flower Moon*. I had been the cinematographer on the last two weeks of his movie *Goodfellas* and wondered if he'd remember me since it had been 30 years. He came over to our table, took a look at me, and said, "Barry. Where's your tie?"

Grazer and I have had several path-crossing adventures in addition to *For Love or Money*. Years later we almost worked together on *Fun with Dick and Jane* until I quit. I was also at a lovely dinner at Grazer's home where Sweetie and I first met Larry and Meg Kasdan, a friendship that would eventually lead to Sweetie and me moving to Telluride, Colorado. Brian's house was formerly owned by Gregory Peck. Brian at some point sold it to Ben Affleck and Jen Garner, who then sold it to Adam Levine, who sold it to Tesla's chief designer, Franz von Holzhausen, who as of this writing, has put it up for sale. That place is like the Liz Taylor of domiciles.

Joel and Ethan's agent, Jim Berkus, who was my agent for a short time until I fired him after the future *Forrest Gump* fiasco, spoke to Grazer and negotiated a fee for the brothers' rewrite. There was one stipulation that made the Coens bristle. Brian would agree to their money demands on the condition that the Coens meet with him.

The brothers have a specific way of writing. They don't work from outlines or index cards push-pinned into cork boards. Nor do they write bullet points on white boards. They mainly pace. The boys start to write and see where the characters and situations take them. In fact, when they were experiencing writers block on *Miller's Crossing*, unable to come up with an ending, they wrote *Barton Fink*, whose main character had writer's block. Only after penning *Fink* did they go back and finish *Miller's Crossing*. More to the point, they are not social animals. Joel and Ethan hate meetings. I had to tell Grazer lunch was a deal breaker.

"Hey, Bri? Look. Joel and Ethan don't want to meet to discuss *For Love or Money*. It's just not how they work. They're kinda shy, they don't plot out their scripts, and feel like they'd just be wasting your time."

"Do they know who I am? Do they know how many movies I've produced?"

"It's not . . . that, Brian. They're huge fans. They have tremendous respect for you. It's just . . . um . . . "

"They've never done a rewrite and I'm offering more money than they probably made on their first three movies combined, and they won't meet me?"

"It's not that, per se, it's just . . . "

"I'm willing to fly to New York."

"And I'm sure they'd really appreciate that gesture, Bri. It's just . . . they're . . . not social. And they don't know what they'll write until they dig into the script. So there'll be nothing to talk about."

"Call them. Tell them we don't have to talk about the script at all. I get that. I respect their process. Tell them to have lunch with me and I will never mention the script. Ever."

"But in that case . . . "

"Tell them I just want to meet them. For lunch. Just meet them."

I relayed the message to the boys.

A couple of days later Joel called.

"Listen, Berkus is going to call Brian. We're not going to have lunch with Grazer, Ba. We just can't. But I promise, it's going to work out. I mean, we only agreed to do it as a favor, so . . . You'll hear from Berkus. That's all I'm saying."

Here's what the Coens agreed to: They would not meet with Brian. In return for that privilege, the Coens waived all their fees, which indeed probably *was* more money than they had earned in their careers.

What makes Grazer a brilliant producer was his takeaway:

While someone giving up serious money to avoid a lunch date might make you a tad depressed, Brian viewed it as a victory. He was such a fantastic producer he got the Coen Brothers to do a rewrite for free.

Although Joel and Eth wrote some great stuff, especially for Fyvush Finkel and Udo Kier, because they were working for free— as a favor to me—they were under no obligation and left the project partway through the rewrite when they got a start date on their next directing gig, which I totally understood.

Graham Place, the producer of the film, and I were grateful for their help and sent the boys a couple of laptop computers. I think they enjoyed the gift more than if we had paid them.

For Love or Money did not do well at the box office. It wasn't a great film. It was, however, one of the best personal experiences I've had as a director.

Danny DeVito Owns Little Italy

Sweetie and I were spending a weekend in New York. It was around 10 PM and we were about to enter The St. Regis hotel on 55th Street between Madison and Fifth Avenues when a limousine, idling in front of the hotel, slowly and mysteriously rolled down its back window.

"Get in!" a voice commanded.

"Hey Danny. Where are we going?"

"DeVito laughed as Sweetie and I piled into the car.

"We're going to Little Italy. It's the San Gennaro festival. We'll get some cannoli."

It was a balmy Saturday night and the streets of Little Italy were teaming with Italians and lovers of Italians. We got out of the limo on Canal and Mulberry Streets.

The thought of walking around Little Italy with Danny DeVito, Mr. Famous Italian American, was daunting. I'm not much of a bodyguard. Sweetie was better than me, but we weren't going to be much of a deterrent to the massive stampede of humanity once they recognized our companion.

Undaunted, as we raced across Canal Street against the light, Danny spotted two cops.

"Hey. Hi. What's your names?"

"I'm Lou. He's Frankie," said the bigger of the two huge cops.

"OK. Until further notice, you're assigned to me. Any problem with that?" asked Danny.

"You got it, Danny. Where to?"

"To get some cannoli," said Danny. "These are my friends. Barry and Sweetie. You're assigned to them too."

As you'd expect, Danny was a big hit. Free cannolis, espressos, pizza everywhere we went.

Danny's plan was to surprise his good friend Cha Cha, who owned a small restaurant on Mulberry Street. Sweetie, Danny, the cops, and I slowly made our way through the crowd ["Hey. Hi. Hey. Howareya? Hiya. Hi"] and into Cha Cha's restaurant. The atmosphere was gloomy. Just a few Italian women in black, sitting around looking glum. In fact, Danny had to knock on the locked door to get us in.

"Where is everybody? Where's Cha Cha? Why are you guys closed?"

"It's his momma, Danny. Cha Cha is down at the hospital. Mother Cabrini's. They think she had a heart attack."

New York's finest gave us an escort back to Danny's limo, still parked on Canal.

"Mother Cabrini hospital," Danny told the driver.

It's now way past midnight when Sweetie, Danny, and I walk into the small neighborhood hospital.

Cha Cha, who had been sitting in the Formica'd waiting room in his finest all white velour track suit, head in hands, elbows resting on his knees, hears some commotion coming from the nurses' station and looks up to see what all the ruckus is about, which is of course, the arrival of Mr. Danny DeVito.

"Danny!" Cha Cha wails.

He stands up, throws open his arms, and reveals himself to be Danny DeVito–sized.

They hug.

"Danny. They won't let me in to see momma."

"Let me see what I can do," says DeVito.

After a whispered discussion between the actor and nurses, Danny comes back and explains to Cha Cha:

"She's in the ICU. They can't let you in right now, but it shouldn't be longer than another hour. They said *I* can go in, so I'll tell momma you're out here."

Ah, to be Danny DeVito.

Sweetie and I hung with Cha Cha, who in addition to being very short, had an extremely big Fu Manchu mustache sitting on a sweet face. Years later we were told by an Italian neighbor of ours, a friend of Cha Cha's from their old neighborhood, that Cha Cha was someone "you don't fucking mess with."

DeVito came out of the ICU, told Cha Cha that momma looked great, everything was going to be OK, and gave Sweetie and me a shout:

"Let's go, Sonnenfelds." We were back at The St. Regis by 2:00 AM.

Only Then, Can the Healing Begin

In need of money to stay afloat, Orion sold *The Addams Family* to Paramount halfway through production. Paramount's chairman, Frank Mancuso, purchased our movie on a Friday morning. Independent of that action, he was fired by the board later that day. Upon viewing the 15-minute sales reel Dede Allen had cut together, Paramount's new chairman, Stanley Jaffe, an unfortunate soul born without a sense of humor, declared our movie uncuttable and unreleasable. The man was so humorless I tried to insert a side letter into my contract for the sequel, *Addams Family Values*, stipulating that Stanley could not attend any recruited audience screenings without his wife, who would tell him when to laugh.

Stanley ordered Paramount president Gary Lucchesi to get a look at the entire film as soon as I was done shooting. I refused. The Directors Guild of America contract protects directors by allocating ten weeks of editing from the end of principle photography until the film is shown to the studio. Gary begged me to at least tell him what the movie was like.

"It's like a much sadder version of *Sophie's Choice*," I replied.

Despite my snarky response, once he saw the first cut, ten weeks down the road, Gary was a happy executive and immediately looked for another movie we could do together.

Gary sent me a paperback copy of *Forrest Gump*, saying there were eight failed screenplays and since none were any good, he was sending me the book instead. He loved the tale and hoped I would too. Perhaps I could crack the story in a way that the producer, Wendy Finerman, and the previous writers hadn't been able to.

In the book, Forrest is a big, heavy, powerful guy. He's famous for it.

I loved the book and knew how to make the movie. I was sure he would say no, but I sent the paperback to Tom Hanks. I had been the cinematographer on *Big*, and we had become friends.

My note to Tom said, "This might be too much like *Big*, in that it's basically another man-child story, but I think we could make the main character really fast instead of huge. Like this guy lives to run."

Tom loved the book and signed on.

Hanks and me on the set of Big.

Wendy and I hired Eric Roth [who would win the Oscar for his adapted screenplay]. His first draft was quite long and had too much voice-over, but was excellent. We had a script, a lead actor, and a studio excited to make the film, which, in the wacky world of my career meant Gary Lucchesi was fired, eventually replaced by Sherry Lansing.

I was close to wrapping production on *For Love or Money* when Sherry decided to make *Addams Family Values*, the sequel to *The Addams Family*. I agreed to do it if she pushed back *Forrest Gump*. I wanted to direct both, and *Addams Family Values* needed to go first, since Christina Ricci and Jimmy Workman—Wednesday and Pugsley—were getting too old for their roles.

Sherry agreed.

Wendy went ballistic.

She wasn't wrong. By delaying *Gump* a year while I made *Addams Family Values*, anything could happen. The studio could change its mind, Tom could quit the project, a similar movie could come out and bomb. . . .

I told Jim Berkus I understood Wendy's point of view, but still wanted to do both.

Here's where it went off the rails:

At the time, Wendy was married to Mark Canton, the executive vice president of worldwide production at Warner Brothers, Hollywood's most powerful studio. Canton called Berkus and said if I did not give up *Forrest Gump*, I would never work in this town again.

"What a cliché," I laughed.

"Seriously, Barry. Do. Not. Fucking. Mess. With. Mark. Canton."

"Jim. The guy's wife is telling her husband, who has nothing to do with this project, to strong arm us?"

"Do. Not. Fucking. Mess. With. Mark. Canton."

Years later I realized Berkus had a much more important relationship with Canton than me. What Jim should have told Wendy was, "You struggled with this project for years and it went nowhere. Barry has signed one of the biggest actors in Hollywood to star in your movie. Wait a year."

On the last day of filming *For Love or Money*, I asked Michael J. Fox what he would do—if he had to choose between *Forrest Gump* or the sequel to my first movie.

"You set the table. Now eat the meal. Do the sequel."

Still undecided, I met Paul Rudnick and Scott Rudin for dinner at the St. Regis Hotel in New York. Paul had been hired to write the screenplay for *Addams Family Values*. The meeting was to convince me to choose the sequel, instead of *Gump*. I had rushed there from our architect's office and showed them blueprints for a substantial house on the water Sweetie and I were going to build in the Hamptons. After I left, Rudin, who knew I'd be paid more for the sequel and knew the house was an expensive undertaking, told Rudnick,

"I own him."

It was not a mistake to choose *Addams Family Values* over *Forrest Gump*.

My mistake—actually, Jim Berkus' screwup, since I had only directed one and a half movies and didn't know the film business, was not negotiating a producing credit on *Gump*. I had supervised a good script and had convinced Tom Hanks to star in the film. That's called producing.

Forrest Gump came out and I was devastated. It got thirteen Oscar nominations, and won six, including best picture.

I fired Berkus.

We stood outside his house. Fake crying he kept repeating, "Look into your heart."

I explained to Jim we weren't friends, we weren't lovers. He was an employee and I was letting him go.

Berkus was the wrong agent for me and I should have known it. I hired him only because he was the Coens' agent. Joel and Ethan don't need an agent to get them work, so his ineptitude didn't and doesn't affect them.

Years earlier, when I hired Berkus to be my agent, he told me, "You need a lawyer."

"I do?"

"I've got a perfect one for you. Melanie Cook. Not only is she a great lawyer, you'll want to fuck her."

I should have fired him on the spot.

Instead, I met Melanie a week later for lunch at the Polo Lounge in The Beverly Hills Hotel and told her what Berkus had said. I also told Woody, Mel's husband.

Scott Rudin and Jim Berkus on the set of The Addams Family.

Sweetie reminded me not to rewrite the past. If I had done *Gump* instead of *Addams Family Values*, we wouldn't have been in LA, and therefore might not have adopted Chloe.

"Yeah, but we wouldn't have known about Chloe and maybe we would have found a treasure chest with a billion dollars, so if your past has Chloe, mine has a billion."

"And . . . ?"

"Yes. Of course. Chloe. I'm just sayin'."

"Don't look back, Barry. You have a good life."

A year later, during Danny DeVito's annual Christmas party at his home in Beverly Hills, I ran into Marty Brest.

Marty was the right guy to ask about *Gump*. He had been fired from or had left several projects that went on to be huge successes, including *War Games*, produced by my future nemesis Walter Parkes.

"How do you deal with it, Marty? I haven't had a good night's sleep since *Gump* came out."

"Have you seen the movie?"

"I can't."

"See it. Only then can the healing begin," he tomed in a very rabbinical way.

I rented a VHS of *Forrest Gump*.

It was not the movie I would have made.

Maybe better.

Maybe worse.

For one thing, mine would have been shorter.

The healing began.

Shut Us Down, Sherry

When we finished shooting *The Addams Family*, Paramount Studios packed and locked the sets in case a sequel was warranted. Packed and locked is the official film business term for storing stuff. The irony of course is that a month before Sherry Lansing green lit *Addams Family Values*, the studio destroyed all the *Addams Family* sets to open up space in their storage facility.

"Hello. This is Sherry Lansing's office. Sherry was wondering if you could stop by at 4 PM today?"

The stupidity of destroying those sets made my conversation with Sherry easy.

"Hi, Sherry, what's up?" I asked as I stepped into her inner office on the Paramount lot.

"Did they offer you water, honey?"

"Got it right here."

"Oh good. Honey: You know I love you. But this movie has just gotten too expensive, and I'm afraid you're going to have to take a million dollars out of the budget or I'll have to shut it down."

The fact that Sherry was using this threat a week before the start of filming made the discussion silly and transparent, and since she employed the same annoying tactic on every Paramount film, I cut to the chase.

"Shut us down, Sherry. If the budget is too high, perhaps Paramount shouldn't have destroyed *millions* of dollars' worth of our sets. So, if there's a problem, talk to yourself. We have the correct budget for this script, given that we now have to build new sets. But with that said, if you have to shut us down, shut us down. I really don't care."

"Honey. Honey. Of course I'm not going to shut you down. I just want you to be responsible. That's all I'm saying. You know that."

"You got it, Sherry. I'll be responsible. May I go now?"

"Honey. Sweetheart. We're on the same team."

"Not really, Sherry."

Not to leave bad enough alone, I became a bigger asshole and added:

"I promise you, Sherry, there's not a penny I can take out of this budget."

"No one is asking you to, honey."

"Sorry. I guess I misunderstood the million-dollar thing. Got it."

I had learned a lot working with Rudin. Almost every studio executive lies and makes threats, but few go through with their ultimatums. In fact, they'll sometimes give in to threats directed at them. I was once meeting Rudin at The Palm restaurant in West Hollywood. It was summer and I was standing on the sidewalk waiting for Scott when he pulled up in his BMW 740i, windows rolled down, yelling into the car's hands-free speaker forcing the valet parker to stand there, holding open the driver's door as Rudin continued his rant:

"It's simple," Rudin screamed. "I either have Maggie Smith or I shut down the movie."

At the time Rudin was not only producing my movie, but also *Sister Act*, written by Paul Rudnick, the same scribe as *Addams Family Values*. It seemed Rudin was passionate about Maggie Smith being in his nun comedy.

"Try it," Rudin screamed.

"If I don't have Maggie Smith, I have no movie."

Over the years, I can't count how many times what was between Scott "having a movie" or "shutting it down" was Maggie Smith.

Given any disagreement, no matter how insignificant, Scott took it right to eleven—right to the edge of the cliff. Don't waste time on the climb, the negotiations, the give and take, just go right to the edge, grab the hand of whatever studio head is not giving in to your outrageous demand, and say, "We're jumping off this cliff together. We are both going to die, but I don't care. I have no children, no one loves me, and if I can't have Maggie Smith in my movie, I have no reason to live." The studio heads usually give in.

Two-thirds of the way through filming *Addams Family Values*, Sherry called Scott and me to her office. With Scott's help, we were over budget and over schedule. I offered to cut a scene scheduled to film the following week that I didn't think we needed. It didn't move the plot forward, wouldn't be missed, and we'd save the cost of a day's shooting.

Since Scott never met an unnecessary scene he didn't love, I was quite surprised and a little suspicious when Rudin offered:

"Sherry. We're going to Anjelica's trailer directly from this meeting to break the news to her. Barry's right. The scene is unnecessary."

Cut to five minutes later in Ms. Huston's camper.

"Anjelica, we are over budget and Paramount is making us take a day out of our schedule, and that scene next week, it just doesn't move the plot forward and we have to get rid of it," I stammered.

Along with "If I don't have [insert your favorite actor here] I have no movie," another Hollywood cliché is:

"The only reason I took this film is because of [insert stupid reason here]."

Here is what Anjelica said:

"The only reason I took this film is because of that very scene."

"It wasn't for the millions of dollars Paramount is paying you?" I queried.

Before Anjelica could answer, Scott spoke up.

"Anjelica. There are three people who matter on this film. Barry. Myself. And you. If you don't want to lose that scene, then we will not lose it."

"That's not what we just agreed to in Sherry's office."

"Barry. Let me handle Sherry."

Ugh.

"Anjelica. You are our partner. End of discussion."

"But . . ."

"Barry. End of discussion."

I wish I could be specific about the scene in question, but for the life of me, I have no memory of what it was. Since it was the only reason Anjelica took the job, we ended up shooting, but not using, it.

Anjelica and Barry stroll the studio lot. Addams Family Values.

What's a Close-up?

Because of the success of *The Addams Family*, and some tough issues Scott was having on *Sister Act*—yes, Rudin did indeed get Maggie Smith—he was less of a presence on the sequel.

He did show up for an early morning rehearsal of a scene in the Addams family graveyard with Anjelica and Raul. Rudin watched the rehearsal, looked at my shot list, and realized that I didn't intend to shoot close-ups. A super wide shot, a tighter two shot, and two sizes of over the shoulders, but no close-ups. Our actors were sitting so close that in order to isolate them, the close-ups would have been extremely tight, something I'm not a fan of.

"You want to hear something funny, Ba?"

"Sure, Scott."

"On my drive to the set today guess who called me?"

"Maggie Smith?"

"Rudnick!"

"About *Sister Act*?" I pretended to naively ask.

"No, that's what's surprising. It was about *our* movie. He asked what scene we were shooting today."

"Really? Rudnick asked you that."

"Weird, right? So I told him we were shooting the romantic scene between Raul and Anjelica in the cemetery, and you know what he said?"

"What, Scott? What did he say?" It was hard to keep a straight face since I knew where he was going.

"Rudnick said, and this really surprised me—'Make sure Barry gets close-ups of Raul and Anjelica.'"

"Wow."

"Right?" said Rudin.

Scott left the set to drive over to Disney to ruin the *Sister Act* director's morning, allowing me to direct the scene without him and without any close-ups. I unclipped my Motorola MicroTAC Ultra Lite cell phone [which was anything but Ultra Lite] from my sagging belt and gave Rudnick a call.

"Hey, Paul. Do you want to know what you did this morning?"

"Sure do."

"You called Rudin."

"I did? What did I say?"

"You asked what scene we were filming today and when Scott told you it was the cemetery scene, you want to know what you said?"

"Absolutely," said Rudnick.

"You told Scott to tell me I should *definitely* get close-ups of Raul and Anjelica."

"Well you better do that, if that's what I told Scott," Paul proclaimed. "And Barry . . . "

"Yes?"

"What's a close-up?"

Too close for close-ups.

The Psychotic Nanny

The wacky and wonderful addition to *Addams Family Values* was Joan Cusack. She is a brilliant actor, and we had great fun working together. Cusack played a serial killer after Fester's fortune.

Film is a fluid, elastic medium. Pull it in one direction and it affects every other part. Dede Allen, *The Addams Family*'s editor, taught me, for instance, that if the third act isn't working, the solution might be to make changes in the second act. Editing a film requires a very holistic approach.

In the case of directing Joan, I didn't know how big her performance should be until the entire show was put together. Joan and I agreed that every scene would have three very different performances. The first version was to play it totally flat with no hint of artifice or wackiness. A deadly professional killer. The second version would be that within her performance, she'd occasionally, accidentally let the audience know that there was something slightly off about her. For the third iteration she'd go full-on nuts and let her inner psychopath be revealed. Joan and I suspected we would use the first, flat, killer performance, but, as I learned from Dede, since you never know until the film is cut together, I'd have options.

I asked Jim Miller, the editor, to use the flattest performance.

It didn't work.

It wasn't fun.

Jim and I started to replace the flat performance with the stranger, somewhat out of control version, and then let loose with Joan's full-on insanity in the third act. Her performance was thrilling.

There is a single moment that should have earned her an Academy Award nomination, although good luck getting a comedy nominated for almost anything. Joan's pulled her car up in front of her mansion. Inside the hideous home is Fester, who she has repeatedly tried to kill. She has rigged the entire house with explosives and is practicing what to say to the police upon their arrival after what will be a huge explosion. The camera is outside the front windshield looking at Joan in the driver's seat.

"But officer," she weeps, "my husband was inside that house." Over the next many seconds, Joan transitions from weeping to laughing hysterically, all in a single take. Brilliant.

Joan Cusack and me. The graveyard. Addams Family Values.

Never Tell the Studio

In Mel Brooks' autobiography, *All About Me!*, he describes filming the musical number "Springtime for Hitler" from his brilliant film *The Producers*. Joseph E. Levine, the producer and financier, was on the set that day. He was already squirming in his chair but when he saw the overhead angle of the chorus line forming a rotating swastika, he furiously objected to the Nazi song's big climax. Joe said it would have to go or he would stop production.

Mel says he told Levine: "Joe. It's out. Don't worry about it."

Mel goes on to say,

"This was the beginning of a pattern for me. Lying to the studio at every turn. On every movie I've done since then, I've often lied when the studio objected to something by saying 'It's out!' but of course, never taking it out. It was always in. Thank God they never remembered."

I felt the climax of *Addams Family Values*, where Joan captures the Addams family, puts them in electric chairs, and gives them a lecture on what drove her to become a serial killer ["Malibu Barbie. That's not what I wanted. That's not who I was."] would need some cutaways from the almost five-minute scene.

I asked Sherry for a small sum to allow second unit to film baby Pubert's adventure rescuing his family. This would give us comic cutaways from Joan's long scene. In addition, Pubert was the motor for the movie's plot, and I feared we had lost track of him. If we didn't set up Pubert leaving his crib and getting to the attic where Joan has corralled the family, Pubert's arrival would seemingly come out of nowhere. Sherry of course refused. I absolutely could not spend any more money, no matter how little, to shoot what I really tried to convince her was a necessary sequence of comedy gold.

"Honey. I love you, but we cannot spend another penny on this movie."

I had learned from my experience on *The Addams Family* that studio executives either do not look at dailies, or if they do, don't know *how* to look at them.

I therefore went ahead and shot the sequence without permission. For two weeks Alan Munro, our visual effects supervisor, filmed the twin girls who played Pubert on various sets. Major shots. Pubert breaks out of his crib, crawls across the floor, and slides down a long banister and knocks a cannon ball into a basement caldron. The cannon ball shoots back up, which seesaws Pubert through the mansion's skylight. We then follow Pubert into space, waving to Wednesday's nemesis, who is on a 727 flying home with her parents, before he lands in the family's attic to save his kin.

Two weeks of filming.

No one from the studio ever questioned all those dailies that were never scripted.

Michael Jackson

Rudin and I had great success with MC Hammer's *Addams Family* end credit tune and we were trying to hook an even bigger fish for the sequel. A Michael Jackson song and video for *Addams Family Values* would amp up the marketing considerably, and so we arranged a meeting.

Because Scott and I were equally unwilling to ride in the other's auto, we each drove our cars the three hours from LA to Michael's home, the Neverland Ranch. We were meeting Mr. Number One. The King of Pop. [We were instructed to *always* refer to him that way.]

It was a beautiful drive, 125 miles along the Pacific Ocean, past Santa Barbara, up curving mountain roads towards Los Olivos. Rudin was driving his black BMW 7 Series with a cracked front windshield. Driving to LAX a week earlier, he had gotten into a screaming match with the studio about some project.

It probably involved Maggie Smith.

Throwing his phone in fury, it hit the windshield with such force the glass spiderwebbed.

It was one of many reasons I wanted to drive myself—I could actually *see* out my window. My red rotary-engined Mazda RX7 held the road as if I was Lewis Hamilton at Silverstone. Or not.

We arrived on time to show the King of Pop our film . . . which meant we were many hours early for his eventual appearance.

Number One "was delayed." We were shown into Michael's screening room, which had a certain vibe.

It was huge. Probably had 50 seats. The giant red velvet draped screen was flanked on either side by ten-foot-tall replicas of the Oscar statues.

The control panel where Michael could dim the lights, run the film, and talk to the projection booth featured a dot matrix panel that scrolled: "MICHAEL JACKSON . . . . #1 . . . . KING OF POP" in a continuous loop, reminding Michael who he was.

Against the back wall on either side of the theater were bedrooms, each with a large single pane picture window providing an expansive view of the screen. Each bedroom had a round, king-sized bed, side tables, lamps, and layers of decorator pillows. Each had its own sound system and intercom to the projection booth. Both also had drapes.

That's all I'm sayin'.

There was only so much time I could sit in the dark with Rudin, who would drop off into a deep subwoofered-non-synco-rhythmic snore for 10 to 30 seconds before he'd go eerily silent. The tension of that quietude was profound, suddenly broken by Rudin's snorting himself back to life followed by the return of deep, troubled snoring.

The past several months had been difficult for the sleeping bear. He was overworked, unable to control his anger [even more than usual], and was suffering [as we *all* were] due to his lack of sleep. Each night his misery was compounded at 2:20 AM, when a mysterious beeping sound would emanate from somewhere within his Hollywood Hills bedroom, waking him from a dead, desperately needed sleep.

Try as he might, he couldn't track down the source of the evil REM-sleep-disruptive beeping. He was convinced it was somehow the satanic doings of his newly installed phone system, and after screaming at enough people [his assistants], he managed to get AT&T to send a technician to sit with him in his bedroom, waiting for the witching hour. At exactly 2:20 AM, the beeping started.

Rudin glared at the technician:

"Are you going to fix this fucking thing?" he barked.

A few seconds later the engineer tracked the sound to one of Scott's bedside tables where Scooter had dumped an unopened box he had been gifted months earlier. Opening the box, they found a watch, its alarm set for 2:20 AM.

Back in Neverland, after several hours of wondering if I was going to be the only witness to Rudin's death by sleep apnea, I spoke up:

"Hey, Scooter. This is nuts."

"Huh?" he startled himself awake.

"Let's get some fresh air. I can't listen to your death rattle anymore."

It was a beautiful day. Neverland was Disneyland-manicured, the sky was deep blue, and colorful flowers in an unnatural display offered 20-foot letters M and J for all to admire. We managed to find the estate's caretaker who had keys to the King of Pop's amusement park.

"Do you want to touch the Yama?"

"Excuse me?" I worried.

"The Yama. Do you want to touch it?"

He pantomimed disturbing circular motions.

"The Yama?" I asked.

"For God's sake, Sonnenfeld. Llama. He wants to know if you fucking want to pet the llama," Rudin howled.

"No, I'm good. Thanks. Just the rides."

Scooter and I deemed the Ferris wheel too risky, but had no problem with the merry-go-round. One of the highlights of my film career was watching Rudin going up and down on a small plastic horsey, trying to hide a grin.

Rudin and I were unaware we were still hours away from Number One's appearance. We were getting hungry, and the King of Pop's estate manager guy must have heard our stomachs growling since there he was, rolling one of those squeaky hotel room service tables towards the front of the screening room building. We got off the merry-go-round and wandered over to the rolling table, that now had folding chairs placed on either side.

The white clothed table was adorned with exquisite silverware. The two plates were covered with silver domes as if presented at a fake fancy restaurant.

"Please," the guy indicated as he picked up the folded napkins, standing by to deposit them on our laps.

Rudin and I each sat on a chair, squinting at the glinting silver domes.

"Mr. Number One. He is still delayed. I brought you some lunch," he said as he placed a hand on each dome.

"Maybe two, three hours, he will arrive. At most."

"Arrive?" I silently mouthed to Rudin, cocking my head.

In perfect sync, our host's estate manager lifted the domes revealing on one plate a chaos of peanut M&M's and on the other, wrapped fun-sized mini Snickers and Kit Kat bars.

"Thank you so much," Rudin chimed in.

"Looks great!" I added.

Years later, producer Jon Peters offered some good Michael Jackson food gossip. When the King of Pop is invited to dinner at a bigwig entertainer's house, Michael insists on bringing his own chef.

While the other dinner guests are forced to dine on ceviche, seared scallops, and rare duck breast, Michael will be found wolfing down his hamburger and fries.

"Just curious," I questioned our stand-in host: "When you say Number One is arriving. From where? Where is he? Like taking a bath or something?"

"Mr. Number One. He's coming from London. But almost here."

The King of Pop showed up a few hours later, never acknowledging his tardiness. It's great to be Number One.

Michael didn't watch much of the movie but agreed to write a song and shoot a music video for us. After a deal was made, sets were built, costumes designed, and a song written. Halfway through filming Paramount's multimillion-dollar video Michael had to leave the country.

In a hurry.

We shipped the set to Michael in Japan. Neither the video nor song were ever finished.

The Mix

The final sound mix is one of the last and most important steps before releasing a movie. It is where the multi-years' worth of effort feels like you've made an actual film.

The mix takes place in a large theater usually on a studio lot. Everyone takes a seat and pretty much lives in it throughout the several weeks of combining and balancing the relationship between music, dialogue, and sound effects.

It is also where we choose between the original recorded [sometimes noisy] production dialogue verses ADR. ADR, automated dialogue replacement, is the re-recorded dialogue done months after production wraps in a quiet specialized studio. A projector plays back the shot in need of improved dialogue recording. Three beeps are played into the actor's headphone and on the fourth, imaginary beep, the actor, hearing the dialogue in his or her headset, and watching the picture being projected, speaks the line in sync with the original picture and sound. Good ADR editors can lift specific words or even syllables from an ADR session so that 90 percent of a line can be as originally recorded on set. I have never worked with her, but I've been told that Meryl Streep will often only speak a word or even a syllable on the ADR stage to save as much of her live performance as possible.

ADR is needed for a multitude of reasons. Sometimes the performance and words are fine, but the use of a wind machine, an airplane flyby, or a truck rumble might have ruined the sound. Sometimes the boom operator misses an actor when she turns her head, or occasionally an actor might slam a car door over the middle of his line, obscuring an important word.

Other times ADR is used to get a different performance—same words, same visual take, just a different attitude. Sometimes we'll use ADR to add off-camera dialogue to clarify something. Or add a funny line on someone's back as they walk away from the camera. The next time you watch Penny Marshall's *A League of Their Own*, a movie I had nothing to do with, check out how many times Penny cuts to the back of someone so she could add a joke via ADR. It often doesn't work, but I applaud the effort.

There are also times when you need to replace an R rated word, whereby "shit" becomes "stuff" or "fucking" becomes "freaking," for the airplane or commercial broadcast TV version. My favorite ADR curse word replacement was on *Get Shorty*, where Dennis Farina's "Fuck you Fuckball" became "Freak you Fuzzball," which was a sentence Farina's character would utter only if he was a mobster from the Church of Latter-Day Saints.

I try to get alternates on the set the same time we film these naughty words, since the pitch and tone and energy come much closer to matching.

One of the weirdest ADR requirements was on Danny DeVito's *Throw Momma from the Train*, when he had to replace Billy Crystal reading a book title—*Fifty Women I'd Like to Fuck*, with *Fifty Women I'd Like to Pork*. While we were filming, Danny was under the impression that he could have one "fuck" and maintain a PG-13 rating, which is weirdly true unless you're using the word "fuck" to describe the physical act of love. Since an R rating was to be avoided to achieve maximum box office, he changed the dialogue from "fuck" to "pork." Unfortunately, since Billy's mouth was speaking an F word, the ADR sounds like Billy is saying "Fifty Women I'd Like to FORK," which sounds even more R rated.

Not all actors are great at ADR: Really good actors can often, but not always, find their voice from half a year ago. Will Smith is excellent. Tommy Lee Jones is excellent. Chris Lloyd, as Fester, could never find his voice again. He was an example of good actor/ lousy ADR.

In the same way a good ADR editor can save or technically enhance a performance, a talented music editor can rearrange cues and lose specific instruments that are competing with dialogue. They can even speed up a piece of music without changing its key.

Addams Family Values was mixed off the Paramount lot at the Todd-AO facility in Hollywood. On the mixing stage were Jim Miller, the editor; Cece Hall, the sound effects designer; Maggie, my assistant; Juno, the ADR editor; Nancy, the music editor; and the three guys who mixed the dialogue, music, and effects—Frankie on effects, Greg [who kept a gun under his seat at the mixing board] on music, and Bob, the dialogue mixer. Sometimes Marc Shaiman, the composer, would show up. And of course, there was the late arrival each night of Scooter-Doody-Rudin.

The Todd-AO mixing stage was bifurcated by a very long mixing board where all three mixers sat. In front of the mixing console were about six rows of movie seats and in front of that, a pool table, a treadmill, and then the movie screen. Some mixing stages substitute a ping-pong table for the pool table. You wouldn't think the noise from either would be such a genius idea, but one of those tables were almost always present. As for the six rows of movie seats, they were a good place to take a nap while pretending you wanted to hear the mix from a different perspective.

Behind the mixing board was a raised platform with a long desk and chairs and lots of electrical outlets. At the back corner was a small room with a window where you could take calls yet still watch and quietly listen to the mix through ceiling speakers; like Michael Jackson's screening room, minus the beds.

In addition to all that sound work, there are two key components that define a final mix: tedium and food.

Choosing where to get lunch and dinner from the two loose leaf books crammed with menus from almost every restaurant in Hollywood—in or out of business—took at least an hour. After that tedious debate was resolved, the endless ordering would begin. There were always a lot of specifics: well-done fries, extra ketchup, lightly toasted, medium rare plus, no onions, extra pickles, no tomatoes unless they're fresh, were some of the demands written on a legal pad passed around the room. Many items were required to be "on the side."

The second time we had to go through the tedious ordering process due to discovering the food establishment originally chosen was no longer in business, I instituted a rule that we had to confirm the vendor was still in operation *before* ordering. That's the kind of take charge director I was.

Complaining that the food hasn't arrived, complaining that it's cold, complaining there isn't enough ketchup, complaining we are ordering too late, complaining that it wasn't fair we're ordering Japanese again, complaining that the Todd-AO provided warm afternoon cookies were late, angry that the twice daily delivery of crudités also provided by the facility was too early or late or had too much celery, me demanding Maggie make a special trip to Popeyes for dirty rice, complaining the portions were too small, or the french dip had too much gristle, took up the rest of the 14-hour days.

The mix is a little like taking a road trip in an old station wagon with too many kids and too many miles; everyone in their pre-assigned seats unable to leave, eating crappy food, playing the same games, hearing the same repetitive stories, eventually arriving at a specific destination. It is also like a car trip in that there is only one driver at a time. All the kids must entertain themselves until one of the mixers wants an opinion of his work.

Half the time I'd say:

"That's still too loud," and the mixer would shoot back,

"Still working on it, boss." [schmuck]

Or:

"Still working on it, sir." [asshole]

There's lots of shooting pool, reading, napping, chatting, and insulting.

Total tedium with moments of compromise and brilliance.

Because almost everything in the film business happens at the very last minute, there is an unmovable date by which you must finish the "print master," the final mix of all the sounds that will be attached to every print. The completion date is sacrosanct; the movie's release date is set in stone. We often worked into the middle of the fucking night. Wrapping past midnight was the norm.

Every evening after about 12 hours of stress, disagreement, compromises, and take-out food, we would have mixed approximately 10 minutes of the movie at which point Scott would be called. He'd eventually arrive, parking in the handicap spot in front of the building. Each night I explained to Rudin that mental handicap-ness did not grant him status to park there but I was ignored.

As we played back our work, yellow pad and Flair felt tipped pen in hand, Rudin would start his notes. The tension would rise, and as one we would shift in our seats as Scott would furiously write another note, followed by the annoying sound of flipping another sheet of paper. Given his one note per page methodology, there were a lot of legal pads that gave their life to our sound mix. A minute or two into playback the nerve-wracking sound of page flipping would stop. This didn't mean Scooter was out of notes. It meant the fucker had fallen asleep.

The beeping watch problem had yet to be resolved, and Scooter was extremely sleep deprived.

Pressing the intercom button to the projection booth I'd say:

"Let's stop for a second please."

The crew would roll their heads against the various couch and chair backs.

I'd brighten the lights and lean my punim within inches of Rudin's tortured REM-deprived face.

"Hey, Scooter!"

Scott would wake up with a start, my impish round face inches from his.

"What?!" he'd bark.

"You fell asleep."

"No I didn't."

The handicap spot Rudin parked in every evening was not well lit. On our last night I snuck out of the mix, opened his unlocked car, turned off the vehicle's overhead light, and put his driver's seat back all the way flat. I walked Scott out at 3:30 AM and watched with glee as he got in his car, sat down, leaned back, and fell flat, flopping awkwardly onto a nonexistent seat back. A juvenile prank that made me very, very happy.

S We Stay. L We Go.

I was at the Wilshire Theatre in Los Angeles with Rob Reiner, his wife, Michele, and Andy Scheinman, a producer and partner at Rob's Castle Rock Entertainment. We were there to see Lily Tomlin's one woman show *The Search for Signs of Intelligent Life in the Universe*. This was around April 1990. I found staying awake difficult. It might have been the venue's heating system.

At intermission I turned to my three friends:

"Should we leave?"

"Leave? Why would we leave?" said Rob.

"It's great," replied Andy.

"In fact, Michele and I already saw the show, and we're watching it for a second time," Rob added.

"You all want to stay?"

"Yes!" said the Reiners.

"You're not just saying that because even though you guys are bored, you don't want to leave because it wouldn't be fair to Andy and me?"

"Are you nuts?" asked Rob.

"OK. Let's take a secret vote," I said, as I ripped a page from my moleskin.

"S we stay. L we go."

"You *are* nuts," cried Rob. "You just this second asked us, and we all said we want to stay."

"I know. Just fill out this ballot. S we stay. L we go."

"Wouldn't it be L we leave or G we go?" asked Michele.

"Right. L we leave."

"This is nuts," Rob announced, shaking his head as he put pen to paper.

I gathered up the four folded ballots, mixed them up in my hands, and started to unfold them.

"OK. We've got an L."

"That's just you," said Rob.

"And a second L," I said.

"One of you voted to go?" Rob asked incredulously.

"And another L.

"And . . . here's the fourth one."

"So what we got here are four Ls," sagely pronounced Rob.

We skedaddled the hell out of the overheated venue, laughing our way up the crowded aisle.

Donald Trump

Mar-a-Lago was the setting for my first in-person introduction to Donald Trump. This was in late 1997. I was in Florida producing and directing *Maximum Bob*, a television pilot for ABC. Elmore Leonard was happy with the movie I directed from his novel *Get Shorty*, and he gave me the rights to *Maximum Bob*, another one of his books. I had never directed for television but thought the book leant itself more to a TV series than a feature film. At the time I had a production company with Barry Josephson, a very helpful executive at SONY where I had directed *Men in Black*. We formed Sonnenfeld Josephson Worldwide Entertainment and made a deal with Disney. Josephson knew Trump [it was hard not to if you were a film producer who might give him a cameo or introduce him to a starlet] and arranged for Sweetie, Chloe, who was four at the time, and myself to visit Don's place for brunch. We were eager to tour the historical mansion he had purchased from the Post Foundation.

So many things were uncomfortable during those two hours, but let's start with the meal. Although Trump had owned the property for a few years, he was now in the process of converting it to a club—makes sense that a "billionaire" would want to share his residence with strangers. We ate in the dining room which was halfway through its renovation. It contained an extremely long gold painted table and several mismatched gold painted chairs. An endless phone cord wandered from a wall jack to the surely important phone sitting on the table in this otherwise empty room, about a 15-foot distance. In addition to the phone, the endless table had a lamp plugged into the opposite wall, which meant another long snake of cord crossing the room. We were offered coffee, pastries, and fruit. In front of Don was a platter of what must have been 80 strips of bacon.

After the meal, our host offered us a tour. First the house, then the grounds. His butler, who had worked at Mar-a-Lago for the previous owner, Marjorie Merriweather Post, was commanded to join us.

"See these bathroom tiles? Mickey and Minnie and Pluto, and . . . um this one. Walt Disney himself painted each and every one of them, isn't that so?" he barked to his validating butler.

"Well, if not Mr. Disney himself, then . . ."

"Walt Disney himself," Don quickly interrupted.

"Let me show you the grounds. You can stay here," he snapped at his butler who had failed the Donald Trump fealty test.

We followed Donald outside.

"You see those tennis courts?" he asked, pointing to his left: "Tennis Court magazine says they're the number one tennis courts in the world."

"Wow," I replied.

"And they should know, right? Let me show you the spa."

As we walked across the property towards the spa construction site, Don offered:

"See this lawn? The one you're walking on?"

"Yeah?"

"Lawn magazine says this is the number one rated lawn in the United States. And as you know, the United States has the best lawns in the world."

"Goes without saying, Donald."

"Look at these magnificent doors," he demanded, as we stood in front of the entrance to the unfinished spa.

"Spa Door magazine calls these the greatest spa doors in the world."

"Spa Door magazine?"

I was about to ask Donald for details when Sweetie gave me a wife kick to the back of my leg. But I was committed:

"*The* Spa Door magazine?"

"*The* Spa Door magazine," Donald proudly confirmed.

On the other side of the property a group of workers were putting up a tent and assembling a carousel.

Trump turned to little Chloe and loomed over her.

"My daughter Tiffany is having her birthday party later. I'm lending her my grounds and paying for the tent myself as a favor to Marla. You should go. You'll have fun."

"That's OK, Donald," I said, rescuing Chloe as she was giving a daughter kick to the back of my leg. "We really have to get going. But thanks for the tour. And those are truly amazing spa doors. I can see why Spa D . . . "

Another wife kick from Sweetie.

My leg was starting to bruise and I needed to get out of there.

"Anyway. Great doors."

The second Donald Trump experience was in 2009. I was directing a very complex Macy's Christmas commercial with many stars who had branded merchandise sold through the store. There was Martha Stewart, Emeril Lagasse, Queen Latifah [who was five hours late the first day and four the second], Usher [who I beat in leg wrestling the last day of the shoot], Jessica Simpson, Mariah Carey, and Donald Trump. I believe Trump was selling his line of menswear, which, I strongly suspect Menswear magazine named best in the world.

All the celebrities were committed full time to our two-day shoot. In addition to tallying nine hours of lateness, the Queen [Latifah] had the driver of her Escalade ram the studio's closed gate while she yelled, "VIP. VIP."

I was told we had Trump for only 20 minutes. I set up a very difficult shot. The camera dollied down the length of a table propped for Christmas dinner with all our stars. It continued to pull back the entire length of the Macy's main floor set we had built on the largest stage at Steiner Studios in Brooklyn. At the end of this long tracking shot, the technocrane mounted camera landed on the backs of Donald Trump and a little girl who is reaching up to touch Don's hair. Turning to the kid in profile, Don threatens:

"Don't even think about it."

"Cut. Great. Let's set up for Donald's close-up. Give me a 27 on a finder."

I was handed the viewfinder with a 27mm lens, and as I lined up the shot, Donald growled:

"You're not shooting me from that side."

"Um . . . "

"That's my bad side. You've got to shoot me from my good side."

"I'm really sorry but the camera angle has to be from here or it won't match what we just shot."

"Find a camera angle that shows my good side, or we're done here, because believe me, you're not shooting me from my bad side and if you can't do that, I'm leaving."

"Got it."

I reached out my hand.

"It was a pleasure working with you."

Donald looked towards the Macy's and ad agency executives:

"You're serious? You're going to let Donald Trump leave without getting a close-up of him?" he said, using his index finger to make a circle around his face.

The execs' worried faces turned towards me:

"Absolutely. And hey. Thanks for coming. It's been a pleasure," I lied, at which point I announced to the crew:

"OK, guys, let's set up for a two shot of Mariah and Martha."

Trump stormed out.

Ten minutes later while lining up the Mariah-Martha two shot I felt a tap on my shoulder.

"You can shoot the close-up from my bad side."

"No need, Donald. We've moved on. But thanks for coming."

"You're serious? Donald Trump is offering you a close-up and you're going to 'move on'?"

"Already have, Donald."

A Broomstick Up His Ass

After I hired Gene Hackman to play schlock movie producer Harry Zimm in *Get Shorty*, I called my former camera operator, Todd Henry, who had worked with Gene on *Class Action*, a film directed by Michael Apted and shot by Conrad Hall.

I wanted some intel from Todd since the first description of working with Gene came from Sam Raimi, via Joel Coen. Joel told me on the first day of filming *The Quick and the Dead*, Sam approached Gene and said something like:

"You're going to walk out the saloon and stop right here. The camera will do a rapid track in on your face. You'll look right, hesitate, then look to your left, come back to center, wait a beat, and leave frame straight ahead exiting close to camera right."

"I'm not doing any of that shit," Gene growled.

"So, Todd," I asked. "Any good Gene Hackman stories?"

"Well, in preproduction both Connie and Apted said they really wanted me involved and encouraged me to talk to the actors, make suggestions about shots, and be another contributor. The very first day, we're filming Hackman sitting behind his desk. The shot starts on Gene, but then he stands and leaves frame. As soon as he gets up, I'm supposed to tilt down onto the desk where we see various legal papers, some of which are clues. I have to pan across these papers slowly, you know, so the audience can read them without the words strobing. Hackman, meanwhile, still off camera, walks behind the dolly then enters frame from the other side of his desk as I tilt up to see his face.

"Gene keeps walking around the camera and entering frame too soon, and since he's off camera, not acting or anything, I asked Gene if he could delay coming back into frame, so I say to Gene, 'Hey, Gene. Can you wait one more beat before you enter frame from off camera. If I pan any faster, the audience won't be able to read the clues on your desk.'

"'Sure,' says Gene.

"'I can also let you shove a broomstick up my ass and wave me around like a fucking monkey, but I'm not doing either of those fucking things.'"

I told this apocryphal story to Steve St. John, the camera and Steadicam operator on *Get Shorty*, warning him if there were any adjustments he needed within a shot, to tell me, and I'd convey the request to Gene. If there's going to be any yelling, better it's directed at me than a crew member.

"Believe me. I am thrilled not to talk to Gene," Steve replied, since this was not the only such story floating around the film industry about Gene's prickly behavior.

We were shooting a very difficult shot in Rene Russo's character's home. In many ways, it was similar to the shot Todd had described. Steve, the camera mounted to his Steadicam rig, had to walk backward down a flight of narrow stairs in an old Spanish style house, pulling Gene in a medium shot. A few steps down the stairs, Hackman looks down and to his right, hearing an off-camera television. As Gene looks towards the TV, his look motivates Steve to pan his camera almost 180 degrees away from Gene, showing Dave Letterman on the TV in the room below. Continuing to walk backward down the stairs, thereby becoming Hackman's moving POV, Steve has to stay on the television long enough for the audience to recognize the show, at which point Steve, still walking down the stairs, pans back to Gene, also continuing to walk towards the camera. The first couple of takes were ruined by Gene getting too close to the camera. By the time Steve panned back to Hackman, it was way too tight a close-up.

Not unlike what happened several years earlier on *Class Action*.

Steve, in the heat of the moment, and with around 60 pounds of equipment strapped to his waist, momentarily forgot the Todd Henry tale from hell and says to Gene:

"Hey Gene. When I pan off you, can you slow down your walk a bit so when I come back onto your face you're a couple of steps further away from the camera?"

As he finished saying this, I tensed up, wishing I could be anywhere but in this room. St. John had realized his mistake right after his "Hey Gene," but was committed and finished his request. He braced for what was about to happen.

And here it comes:

"Sure," said Gene.

Wool Shirt

At some point during preproduction Hackman called me from his home in Santa Fe. He suggested Harry Zimm, Gene's character in *Get Shorty*, have fake capped teeth that were way too white. I loved the idea and added a gold chain with the Jewish letter "Hei" on it. Gene suggested Harry, the schlock producer/director, thought himself a bit of an artist and should have a goatee. I had never seen Gene with facial hair, so I said,

"Yeah. Maybe. Why don't you grow one and we'll look at it together when you get to LA."

"I'm not going to fucking waste my time growing a goatee if you're not going to fucking use it in the film," Gene, racing from zero to a thousand in about point six seconds, screamed. "Forget it!"

Although I said, "You're absolutely right Gene. I love the idea. Definitely grow it," here's what I actually was thinking:

"How hard is it to *NOT SHAVE*?"

I figured if I hated it, I'd deal with his facial hair in person.

Gene arrived in LA a month later. His goatee, fake capped teeth, and "Hei" were brilliant.

Goatee, capped teeth, gold "Hei" chain. Get Shorty.

We started filming on a Monday morning, beginning with a short sequence with Rene Russo and Gene, then got ready for the first scene of the show with Hackman and John Travolta. Gene was a professional, memorizing his lines before showing up on the set.

In fact, he had a unique script.

A week or two before starting a film, Gene cuts and pastes his screenplay, removing any descriptions or stage direction that a writer adds to help the studio understand a character's action, emotion, or motivation. While a writer might type "'Go to Hell,' *Harry screamed furiously*" in Hackman's script, it just read: "Go to Hell." He didn't want any fucking shithead writer telling him to *scream furiously*, unless that was a choice *he* made.

The two actors, cinematographer, prop person, assistant director, script supervisor, and I had a closed set rehearsal. After working on the scene, we'd open it up to the rest of the crew to watch a final rehearsal at which point the actors would get into hair, makeup, and wardrobe. The grips and electrics would light and put the camera in position.

Travolta and Hackman were about to shoot their first scene together.

"Hey Gene. How was your weekend?" a charming John Travolta asked a very professional, intimidating Gene Hackman.

"Well, with eight fucking pages of dialogue, I pretty much spent the whole fucking weekend memorizing today's work."

"That's a waste of a weekend," replied the charmer.

"Uh oh," thought the director.

Indeed, Hackman was off book knowing every line of dialogue. John, on the other hand, probably hadn't read the script since his agent made his very lucrative deal. Fumbling his lines, or forgetting them entirely, I could tell John had no idea how angry Gene was getting. I knew we were in for a very, very long day. What I didn't know was that in an hour my wife would be in tears and the crew would be on the lawn playing frisbee, taking naps, and drinking coffee.

The actors went to hair, makeup, and wardrobe, and the crew lit the scene. Sweetie, an associate producer on the show, stopped by the set, which was high in the hills of Malibu overlooking a sparkling Pacific Ocean.

There are a variety of reasons why I direct standing or sitting next to the camera. Being close to the actors allows me to be an immediate audience. As soon as I call "cut," I can step in and give notes. I get a better sense of performance viewing the actors live than on a monitor. Sitting around "video village," as it is called, with producers, studio executives, and crew members, watching the actors on a television screen, can make you lazy, plus you are frequently offered unwanted advice.

My director's chair is a saddle on wheels. The saddle makes me sit up straight and is much better on my back than a sagging canvas director's chair. The twelve wheels [three on each corner] offer comforting stability and allow me to race up to actors without having to stand.

Me and my saddle. Night shoot. MIB3.

The camera was set up for a two-shot master, which meant we saw Hackman and Travolta in the same frame. For almost any film, but especially comedies, you want the actors to talk fast. Comedies play best in master shots. Action and reaction in the same frame. The more you have to cut to different angles to create pace and performance, the more your comedy isn't funny. Pace should be created on set, not in the cutting room.

Playing a scene in a master shot obviously requires both actors to *know their lines!*

Unfortunately, while Hackman spent his weekend learning his, who knows what John was doing. Gene's performance was fantastic, John was slow on the uptake and he fumbled and mumbled through the scene. Hackman was getting more and more frustrated with John's delayed responses and lack of pace.

The camera assistant announced he had to reload the camera and while that was happening, I got off my saddle and walked from the set over to Sweetie who was watching the takes from video village.

"Hackman is fantastic, isn't he?"

"Just great," Sweetie replied. "Really great."

"Loaded," the camera assistant announced.

I walked back to the set.

"Roll camera," I said. "Oh, and Gene, stand up a sentence earlier on this take. I think it will be funnier. And, action."

At which point, Gene, instead of speaking the dialogue as written, screamed:

"You know what? Cut the fucking camera. You truly don't have a fucking clue, do you? You'll take advice from anyone. You'll take direction from your own fucking wife! Don't you have any goddamn opinions of your own?"

I turned to the first assistant director:

"Check with the caterer. See if they're ready for lunch."

"Ready for lunch? They won't be ready for at least three hours."

"Ask them."

I was looking at Sweetie. She was mortified, with tears welling up in her eyes.

"Two hours, if they rush."

"OK, everyone," I heard myself say. "That's lunch."

As Gene was fuming towards the front door, I stopped him:

"Hey, Gene. One second. Just so you know. If it helps to yell at me this entire movie, go ahead. It doesn't bother me at all, so keep screaming."

"What the fuck are you talking about?"

"I know you're not angry at me. You're angry at John for not knowing his lines and you can't yell at him, since you've got to work with him for the next ten weeks. You know my wife didn't tell me how to direct, and I know you need to yell at someone, so yell at me. But please leave Sweetie out of it."

Hackman uttered the terrifying words that still give me shivers 29 years later:

"Come to my camper. We'll have lunch."

In addition to directing Gene Hackman once, I've directed Tommy Lee Jones three times. In many ways, they're the same guy, although they'd hate to hear that. Rumor has it they despised each other while working on *The Package*.

Gene and Tommy are both manly men: Gene flies airplanes and was a race car driver. Tommy is a cowboy. They also both happen to be great actors, and that throws them off. They hate being fussed at. They're not comfortable playing "dress up." They dislike people putting makeup on their faces, having lint picked off their clothes. But there they are, two manly, highly paid actors. These contradictions lead to self-hate.

Sitting in Gene's trailer, preferring to be anywhere but here, Hackman tells me he wears a hair shirt [a garment made from rough animal hair, usually goat, designed to make the wearer—usually British—uncomfortable]. Gene is in constant, self-loathing pain. Fine for him, not so great for Barry. He tells me how much he hates himself, how hard it is to be him, and how angry he always is.

Travolta and Hackman had other run-ins, but in every case, John was oblivious to Gene's frustration and I took the brunt of his fury.

The second incident was the next day, also at the Malibu house. I realized the only way I was going to have any pace, any chance of staying on a master shot, was to write giant cue cards for John. I had never done this before or since, but it helped.

Hackman, Travolta, and Rene Russo are in Rene's dining room. At one point John asked me where we were starting from, and before I could answer, Gene, pointing to the cue cards, said, "Right here, John.

"Right at the top of your cue card." John didn't realize Gene was making fun of him. Since Gene's anger in this one incident wasn't directed at me, I thought it was funny.

The first of many scenes with cue cards.

Not so funny was the last of Gene's fury, once again with me as foil. We were filming at Abiquiu, a fancy southwest restaurant in Santa Monica. It was a difficult day with a lot of different setups, including a scene that had John pulling Jim Gandolfini's stunt double down a flight of stairs. The location was a very expensive rental and our hours were limited. We bought out their lunch service but had to be out by dinner.

Unfortunately, Travolta had been nominated for an Academy Award for *Pulp Fiction* and he decided today was the best time to have various clothing designers offer up their options for his free tuxedo wearing at the Oscars. Hackman, Rene Russo, Gandolfini, and Delroy Lindo were cooling their jets far too long waiting for John to come out of his camper. My sciatica was raging. Finally, after the third time we knocked on his camper door, John came to set.

I have never worked with anyone who loved being a movie star as much as John Travolta. I'm not saying he didn't also love acting, but he truly loved the fame and glamour and all things that Tommy Lee Jones and Gene Hackman hated.

John is charming and not self-aware. He arrived on set for the rehearsal with no sense that he had kept everyone waiting. He preceded to ask the cast their thoughts about various clothing designers.

Gene had no opinions.

We finished a rehearsal, I dismissed the cast, and mentioned to the cinematographer and script supervisor that when we went in for Gene's close-up, his looks to John would be the wrong screen direction and we would need an additional angle where it would be correct. Gene overheard me and, with the previous license I gave Hackman to yell at me, and given how furious he was at John, Gene started screaming:

"Find a fucking camera angle where *all* my looks work. I'm not doing a scene where only some of the fucking shot works."

"The truth is, Gene . . . "

"In my entire fucking career, I have never worked with a more clueless, inept director."

"Actually, Gene . . . "

"Never have I done a shot where only some of my looks were usable."

"You know, Gene. Pretty much every day you've been on a movie set there have been camera setups where some of your looks were in the wrong screen direction."

"Bullshit. Find a camera angle where *all* my looks work."

"OK. Found it. Go get dressed and made up, and when you come back the camera will be in a place where all your eye-lines are in the proper direction."

I knew Gene would calm down now that he had vented. I also suspected he would forget our discussion about screen direction, which is exactly what happened.

Farina's Fears

I loved Dennis Farina. Dennis was a handsome retired cop when Michael Mann hired him to be a consultant, then an actor, on his television show *Crime Story*. He first came to my attention as the mobster in *Midnight Run*: "Am I talking to moron number one or moron number two?" Dennis is the kind of actor that when you read a new script, you think: "Where's the role for Farina?" I feel the same way about Patrick Warburton. Both were great in *Big Trouble*, a movie I directed in Miami Beach several years after *Get Shorty*.

During a long lighting setup on *Get Shorty*, Dennis and I had a chat. I knew from earlier conversations he split his time between Scottsdale, Arizona, and his hometown of Chicago. Since he was a Chicago police detective for 20 years, I asked if he was around during the '68 Democratic National Convention. He was, but he wouldn't tell me much about his experience since he wanted me to like him and "You might have a problem with all the fuckin' shithead hippies' skulls I fuckin' bashed in." He also had served papers on Bernardine Dohrn, the former leader of the Weather Underground who was on the FBI's 10 Most Wanted List.

"So, like, when you go back to Chicago, do you mainly hang out with your old police department friends?"

"Well, in all honesty, Ba. Most of my friends are on the other side."

"I see."

Yikes.

During an endless three seconds of stupidly nodding my head, taking in this new information, I desperately tried to come up with another question. *Any* question. I tossed him a non sequitur:

"So, Dennis. In your life. Have you ever been afraid of anyone?"

"Yeah. Sinatra. No one wanted to be near Frank if he was in a bad mood. When Frank spoke, the room snapped to attention. And *everyone* avoided eye contact."

"Was Sinatra the coolest guy you ever met?"

"Nah. The guy that everyone wanted to be, including Sinatra, was Dean. Martin was by far the coolest guy ever."

"So Sinatra was the only guy you've ever been afraid of?"

"Maybe one other guy, Ba. But the jury's still out on him."

Dennis played mobster Ray Bones. We were about to shoot a scene in Harry Zimm's office, a small set built in a crappy little studio on the west side of Los Angeles. We had already shot the beginning of the scene, where Harry, conjuring his inner Chili Palmer [Travolta's character], tries to convince a very pissed off Ray Bones to invest 300 grand in Harry's film. Having just finished the shot where Ray smashes Harry in the face with a telephone, we were now ready for the stunt where Ray flips over Harry's desk, grabs him by his shirt collar, proceeds to bounce him off several Venetian blinded windows, shoves him hard into a bookcase, and finally tosses him violently onto the floor. I wanted the stunt to be sloppy and real, shooting it in one continuous take without coverage.

Although we used Farina, we had Hackman's long-time stunt double and former professional baseball player, Whitey, stand in for Gene. Whitey was an excellent match for Hackman, and since the lighting was backlit from the windows, putting Whitey in semi-shadow, and the shot pretty wide, it was going to work out great.

Farina and Whitey rehearsed a couple of times at half speed, and we were ready for the shot.

I felt a cold breeze on the back of my neck, which as I feared meant Hackman had arrived uninvited, to watch the stunt.

We shot two perfect takes and I was ready to move on when Hackman tapped me on the shoulder.

"You want me to do one?"

"No, that's OK, Gene. Whitey's a pretty great match for you, he's backlit, and I think Dennis would hold back if he was throwing you around instead of Whitey."

"Go ask him."

"It's OK, Gene. I don't need you to do it."

"Ask him."

"It's just that . . . "

"Go fucking ask him."

"Yeah, sure Gene."

I took Dennis off set.

"Hey Dennis. I told Gene we didn't need it, but Gene wants to do the stunt."

"No. No. No. Please. Don't let him do it. I might hurt the guy and he's really big and probably could beat the shit out of me and then just to protect myself I gotta go shoot him and now I'm the guy who shot Gene Hackman. Seriously, Ba. Don't let him."

So Gene was the other guy, besides Sinatra, Dennis Farina was afraid of.

I told Hackman Dennis preferred working with Whitey and I was happy with the two takes we already shot.

Hackman never knew it, but that afternoon I may have saved his life.

Dennis Farina with fake broken nose.

The Trouble with Words

Memorizing dialogue is a pain for any actor, but for Travolta, it was particularly difficult. John struggled with words. He would offer excuses for not knowing his lines, usually blaming the script.

I was at dailies at MGM when John called my house and cried to Sweetie:

"He's making me learn too many words. Tell Barry to lose words. It's too many. I can't learn them."

I called John when I got home and listened to his weeping.

"How many words are too many words, John? How many words of tomorrow's scene do you want me to lose?"

"Six."

"Six? You're saying if we lose six words, you'll know the scene tomorrow?"

"It would help."

"Let's read the scene together. Right now. Maybe we need to lose twenty words. Or twelve. Or fifty. Or maybe you'll want to keep all of them after we read it together."

"Don't play mind games with me, Barry. Just pick six words."

"Well, let's read the scene anyway. Maybe we'll find words we *both* want to lose."

"I don't have a script at the moment."

"Right, but, how are you going to memorize tomorrow's . . . "

"Please. Please. Just pick six words."

"Do contractions count as losing a word?"

"Contractions?"

"Like if I change 'do not' to 'don't' does that count as losing a word?"

"Yes."

"Except Chili wouldn't say 'don't.' He'd say 'do not.'"

"Six words Barry."

"Right, but you don't have a script with you? At your house? To memorize it?"

"I'll get my assistant to fax the scene over to me. Later. After dinner."

"Dinner? It's like ten . . ."

"Six words."

I lost a line of dialogue that was eight words. John was quite happy, except the next day he was working off cue cards.

At the end of another frustrating day, I'm sitting with Travolta in his camper:

"So John. You have tomorrow off and Monday's a holiday, which means four days without work. Tuesday, we have a really hard scene. It's got a big page count and we only have the Presidential Suite at the Century Plaza Hotel for one day. You need to know the dialogue. You can't be fumbling for words. I want to play a lot of the dialogue in master shots and don't want to edit the scene into a million pieces to tighten up your performance. You've got to come in next week knowing your lines. So, let's read the scene now, and you tell me if there's anything you think you'll have trouble with."

We read the scene together. John was in a hurry to get home and said all the words were fine. He'd memorize everything. I made sure he took two copies of the script home with him. I also had an additional two copies dropped off at his house.

Tuesday morning it was immediately clear John had not even glanced at his script over the past four days. We rehearsed and rehearsed and the words just wouldn't come. I showed the scene to the crew with John reading from his script and we started to light, sending our actors off to hair and makeup.

Ten minutes later, Graham, the co-producer, found me on set.

"We've called for the doctor. For Travolta. He's not feeling well."

"Great."

We kept lighting since even if we had to shut down and put in for an insurance day, we could be pre-lit for whenever John felt better. Or perhaps John would get a B_{12} injection and suddenly not only feel great but magically know his lines.

The doctor examined John then came to talk to Graham and me.

"What's up, Doc?"

"I couldn't find anything wrong physically. His vitals are all fine. No temperature; pulse, blood pressure all OK. There is one thing. One thing that might be causing his illness. Something John asked me to help him with."

"Oy."

"I think it would help John's health if he didn't have to learn so many words."

"OK, Doctor. Thanks for that. But here's the thi . . ."

Graham interrupted, knowing it was a waste of time to get into this debate with a doctor.

"Can he work today? Is he capable?" Graham asked.

"You'll have to check with Mr. Travolta."

I went down the hallway to the room we had rented for John. He was lying on a couch with a wet hand towel over his eyes. He would have made my mother proud.

"I'm sorry you're not feeling well, John. Is there any chance we could shoot your off camera angles with you reading from the script? And maybe, by doing that, you'll learn *your* lines, and we could shoot the master and your coverage later in the day? Do you think that's worth a try?"

"Maybe," he said, like a wounded 5-year-old who knew he was in trouble.

"Well, let's give it a try. Take your time. Relax a little. Maybe look over the script if it doesn't make you sick. Then go down to hair and makeup and wardrobe, and we'll see how it goes. OK?"

"OK. I guess. But, Barry."

"I know, John. Too many words."

Somehow, we got through the day. My desire to shoot the scene in master, or two shots, went out the window, and in spite of my dreams, the scene was edited exactly how I hoped it wouldn't be. Too many cuts.

Editing is a magical alchemy. Throughout preproduction a director has plans and aspirations. Sunsets, clear blue skies, fast talking actors, stunts that look real, mechanical gags that actually work . . .

Then you start making the movie. Everything goes wrong. Sunset scenes are overcast. Blue skies become rain. Fast talking actors are rare. You're now done filming and the movie is as bad as it will ever be. Editing is where you get to make it better.

One of the most amazing tools in postproduction is the manipulation of dialogue. Editors can use pieces of audio from one take and put it into a different visual take where the camera move was better, the diction clearer, or the performance more moving. In the case of Travolta's performance in *Get Shorty*—a performance that won John a Golden Globe—something like a third of the words you hear are from a different audio take than the visual one. There are dozens of on screen "ah"s and "um"s that we removed. His mouth still makes the "ah" or "um" movement, but the audience doesn't hear it, and unbelievably, doesn't miss it.

There were a few places where we were going to need ADR, either to smooth out the dialogue jenga of different takes, or because of traffic or airplane noise.

John refused to do ADR until he saw the movie. I relented and arranged for a screening.

His agent, Fred Westheimer, called:

"John saw the movie and loves it. He feels his performance is perfect and doesn't want to give you the chance to ruin it by doing unnecessary ADR."

Less than calmly, I said:

"Guess what Fred: What John saw isn't *his* performance. It's *mine*. Travolta has no idea how many dialogue edits there are in every single sentence. There are multiple sound takes in every fucking line of his fucking dialogue. If it weren't for Jim Miller [the editor] and me, there would be no performance to ruin. Tell John he better get into that ADR studio or I'll put back his actual performance."

John squawked but came in to loop the sentences I needed. With *Pulp Fiction* and now *Get Shorty* under his belt, like a phoenix, he had risen.

No Fucking Clue

Gene Hackman hates himself so much that he can't watch any movie he's been in. On the set one morning, he told me I was lucky he even showed up, since he had accidentally seen a few seconds of himself in *The Poseidon Adventure* the night before on television.

In addition to *Get Shorty*'s big West Coast Premiere at Mann's Chinese Theatre, we had a smaller East Coast screening in New York City at the Museum of Modern Art.

Just before the movie started someone in the seat directly behind me tapped my shoulder. I knew it couldn't be good because my shoulder froze—as if someone had sprayed lidocaine on it. I turned around and it was Gene Hackman, sitting next to our mutual agent, Fred Specktor.

"Listen. I never come to these fucking things. I'm doing Fred a favor so you have some movie people at your premiere. I'm not staying so don't take it personally that I'm gone when this thing is over."

"No problem, Gene. Thanks for coming."

The movie ended, there was another tap and another frozen shoulder. *Hackman was still behind me.* It may be the only movie Gene ever saw himself in.

"It's great. *He's* great," Gene whispered.

"Weird, huh?"

"I can't fucking believe it."

The after party was a lot of fun. I got to sit next to Stockard Channing. It was all fantastic until my shoulder, for a third time that night, froze.

"I was going to write you a letter but that's chickenshit so I'm telling it to your face. Let's go."

Gene and I walked to a quiet corner of the room, and this is what he said:

"The movie is great. Really well done."

"Well thanks, Gene, I mean . . . "

"Let me finish."

"Sorry."

"Your film is great. It's that simple. And here's the thing: I could have been so much better."

"You were really good, Ge . . . "

"Stop interrupting! Just listen, God damn it. What is wrong with you? I'm trying to tell you, I could have been so much better, except the entire time I was working on this show, *I DIDN'T THINK YOU HAD A FUCKING CLUE.*"

"Thanks, Gene."

Additional *Get Shorty* Fun Facts

Before we leave *Get Shorty*, here are a few more fun facts in no particular order:

I initially thought the score for *Get Shorty* should be jazz. I liked John Lurie's work and thought he would be a "hip" choice. After I hired him, but before we started to spot the areas that needed his music, Jim Miller, the editor, was ready to show me his first cut of the movie. This is called the "editor's cut," which is done without the input of the director. Graham, the co-producer; his wife, Beverly; Sweetie, and I watched the film at the Broadway Video screening room in the Brill Building near Times Square. As per my request, Jim had added a temporary score using jazz.

Everything about the film was terrible. The show was too slow, the performances were flabby, and the music did not give the film any energy or drive. It was truly one of the most depressing days of my career; like a not getting out of bed for two weeks kind of depression. We eventually got the film in good shape but realized that a jazz score was without energy and lacked musical themes or a motor. I explained my concerns to our composer so he would be aware of what the film needed before he started.

Unfortunately, John hadn't done much film scoring and his compositions, like the man himself, tended to wander in various directions. In addition, he didn't write to dialogue. He would add instruments and crescendos just as two actors might start to whisper. It's as if he started writing a piece based on the scene, but soon forgot his assignment, getting carried away by his own cool sounds, with no thought to what the scene needed.

Luckily, we had a great music editor—Bobby Maxton. A handsome guy with piercing blue eyes, Bobby has since worked on most of my films, usually as the dialogue editor. But on *Get Shorty*, Bobby was editing the music and managed to take Lurie's tracks and lose some instruments, cut out whole sections, move themes around, and make the music work much better with dialogue. Between Bobby and Booker T. and the MG's—and let's face it: there isn't a scene in film history that wouldn't be improved by "Green Onions"—the score was nominated for a Grammy and won an ASCAP award.

John hated me. I was as specific as he was loose and fancy free. He titled his album tracks "I hate you Barry." "Fuck you Barry." And "Barry Sucks." The record label stepped in and changed the titles before the CD was released.

⋆　⋆　⋆

Early in preproduction my fellow producer, Danny DeVito, and I decided Rene Russo might make a great Karen Flores, the Queen of B movies, known for her great scream. Danny and I took Rene to lunch at the Peninsula Hotel in Beverly Hills, where I was staying. Rene is lovely. Sweet and personable, charming and beautiful. She ordered the tuna niçoise. In a shy adorable way, Rene quietly asked our waiter if there was by any chance sesame oil in the salad since she was highly allergic. She didn't want to be one of those Hollywood actors ordering things on the side, or making it all about her, but she was deathly allergic to sesame and just needed to make sure. The imperious waiter assured her there had never been such an item in the Peninsula's niçoise—and you already know where this story is heading.

Our food arrived.

I was sitting opposite Rene.

"I know the waiter said there was no sesame oil in this, but I feel a little funny. On the other hand," she continued as she scratched her neck, "if there was sesame oil in the salad, I'd be scratching like crazy and I'd be breaking out in a rash."

"Hey, Rene," I said. "You're scratching like crazy and your face is totally splotchy."

At this point, in perfect comic timing, the pompous waiter races into frame, grabs Rene's plate, and says, "Oh my God. Oh my God. I am so sorry. I am so sorry."

Cut to my room at the Peninsula. The hotel has called a doctor, who is now examining Rene on my bed. Danny and I are sitting on the couch listening to the intimate details of Rene's health history.

"Age?"

"Forty."

"Do you have regular periods?"

"Hey, Danny. Maybe we should wait out in the hallway."

"Nah. This is just getting good, Ba."

At this point Rene's husband, Dan, arrives. The doc gives Rene a shot of antihistamine, announces she will live, and Rene becomes our Karen Flores.

★   ★   ★

Delroy Lindo's acting technique involved belching out a very loud, very deep "Uuuuuummmmmmaaaaaaaahhhhhhhh."

Before every take.

By the end of the show, it was common for Delroy's vocal exercise to illicit cow mooing sounds from the crew. Delroy insisted on calling me BARRY SONNENFELD. Perhaps he learned this in acting school along with his "Uuuuuuuummmmmaaaahhhhhh" vocalizations.

Delroy also had a real love of props, something that drives me crazy. Getting overly involved with props tends to be self-indulgent and slows down a performance. Don't get me started on Nicolas Cage and his fucking shoehorn in *Raising Arizona*.

In the climactic scene of *Get Shorty*, Travolta arrives at Delroy's house, a kidnapped Rene Russo in his bathroom. Delroy has demanded that Travolta bring him the briefcase with 300 grand or he kills Rene. We rehearsed the scene. Delroy held on to the briefcase the entire time.

"Hey Delroy. Put the briefcase down before you head outside to the balcony. We don't want you holding on to it when you're out there."

"I wouldn't do that, Barry Sonnenfeld. I would not put down that briefcase."

"Why's that, Delroy?"

"This whole movie is about me trying to get that money. Now that I have it, I wouldn't let it go."

"Delroy. You are in your own home. You've got a gun. You've got Gandolfini, who also has a gun, so you're pretty damn safe. There is absolutely no reason to hold on to the case. Plus, you are not, I promise, going to want to hold that briefcase through this very long scene, especially once you're on the balcony and need to get physical, let alone be tossed over the railing, leaving the briefcase up here. It's just going to complicate the blocking and make you look silly."

"Barry Sonnenfeld. I would not, my character would not, let go of this money. It is my whole raison d'être."

"I swear, Delroy. You do not want to act this entire scene holding a fucking briefcase."

"I do, Barry Sonnenfeld. I do."

Now I turn into a fed-up parent.

"OK, Delroy. You can hold the stupid briefcase. But here's the thing, buddy [I so wanted to call him Delroy Lindo but didn't think he'd get the joke]. Do not. Do not come to me halfway through this scene and whine, 'Oh, Barry Sonnenfeld. I don't want to hold this briefcase anymore. You were right, Barry Sonnenfeld. Can I put the briefcase down now? Please?' because once we start shooting this scene, you are stuck holding on to that stupid fucking briefcase."

"I would never do that Barry Sonnenfeld. I would never want to drop this briefcase. I promise you that. I would never, ever, want to put down this briefcase."

Pretty quickly, Delroy realized how wrong he was. Before lunch he was practically crying, begging me to let him put down the case.

I knew this would happen and had a plan that allowed him to drop it.

"You're the man, Barry Sonnenfeld."

Jim and Delroy. Delroy refuses to put down the bag of money.

I had a similar, but not as annoying discussion with James Gandolfini, who played Bear, a former stunt man and present bodyguard to Delroy. Jim decided all stunt men are from North Carolina and would have a Southern accent. I warned him that a Southern accent would slow down the pace of his dialogue. He'd talk too slow. Gandolfini promised he could and would talk fast. I knew he'd never live up to his promise. Each time I asked him to pace it up, he'd explain there's a certain rhythm to a Southern accent, which is exactly why I didn't want him to have one.

When the movie came out, he apologized.

"You were right, Ba."

"Thanks, Gandolfini. A little late, but sure."

★   ★   ★

The last scene of the movie, not in the book, totally invented by Scott Frank, the film's screenwriter, involved an audience fake out. At first we think we are at LAX about to see Ray Bones get arrested, but we quickly discover that Chili has actually become a Hollywood producer, and what we are watching is the movie version of his experience in Hollywood. Harvey Keitel played Ray Bones; Penny Marshall, the director; and DeVito played Chili in the movie within our movie. Rene Russo, Bette Midler, and Gene Hackman played Chili's other producers.

The scene was going to be photographed in one long Steadicam take and would require several hours of lighting. After the rehearsal I kicked myself for not hiring an actress who could scream, kicking off the elaborate camera move, mirroring Rene Russo's character in our movie.

Hackman overheard my lament and said, "I have the perfect actress for you. She's great. Exactly what you're looking for. Donna Scott, Tony Scott's wife. But if I make the call, don't get her down here and not fucking use her. Don't waste her fucking time. If I call her, you're going to treat her with fucking respect."

Donna showed up to my trailer an hour later, beautiful, in self-done hair and makeup ready to go. She brought a series of choices for her wardrobe. As she laid her outfits on the couch, she gave me a running commentary:

"Cute.

"More corporate.

"Possibly a little too 'night out' for an airport terminal.

"Oh. This red one makes my boobs look really big."

"Red works," I said.

Donna was fantastic.

Donna Scott. Danny DeVito. The movie within a movie.

Penny Marshall made sure I knew she was doing this cameo as a favor for Danny, not for me, even though I was the cinematographer on her hit *Big*.

"Just so ya know," she mumbled, "I'm doing this for Danny, not you."

"Got it, Pen. Thanks for helping out Danny. I'm sure he appreciates it."

Harvey Keitel, also doing Danny a favor, agreed to do this one shot, but the first few takes he barely spoke his one line of dialogue:

Ray Bones' iconic "Fuck you, Fuckball," which of course became "Freak you, Fuzzball" for airplanes and broadcast TV.

"Hey, Harvey. Can you not whisper the line? I need you to speak it out."

It was at that moment I discovered Keitel thought he was coming down to do a silent bit and would not have done it if he knew he was speaking. I convinced Harvey that since he was already here, doing Danny a favor, he might as well go all the way and actually speak, which he eventually did.

Harvey Keitel and me sporting a spare mustache.

★   ★   ★

On the first day of shooting, Elmore Leonard asked if I would let the real Chili Palmer, who was one of Elmore's researchers, be an extra in the scene. He would play a non-speaking mobster, one of Dennis Farina's buddies, eating at the same Italian restaurant where Travolta is dining. After John met the real Chili Palmer, he angrily took me aside:

"Why didn't you tell me there was a real Chili Palmer? I would have studied him. Hung out with the guy for a few weeks. Follow him around. Pick up some mannerisms."

"John. He's a name. Not a character. The real Chili isn't a mobster. He's Elmore Leonard's researcher. He talks slowly and has a limp. What about him would you copy?"

"I guess you're right," Travolta admitted. "But next time, let me know."

"You got it, John," I said.

"Next time I'll let you know."

Travolta, Farina, John's stand-in, and the real Chili Palmer, far right.

The Anti-Christ

The last recruited audience screening of *Get Shorty* was in San Jose, California. MGM chartered a jet to take chairman Mike Marcus and his execs, Danny DeVito and his Jersey Films' team, Joe Farrell, the CEO of the National Research Group, and me from Van Nuys to the movie theater in San Jose.

Farrell's company, NRG, was hired by all the studios as a marketing and research consultant. He is now deceased, but in his lifetime he did more to ruin movies than almost anyone. Various obituaries called him "a power broker," "guru," and "Godfather of the film business," three adjectives describing the exact opposite of what you'd want in an unbiased, objective researcher.

NRG recruited the audience for, and ran the screenings of films in progress. The audience was given cards after viewing the movie asking both helpful and leading questions. NRG would tally this information in real time and make suggestions. Often, if the studio and director were having disagreements, the studio might ask Joe to include specific questions to help get the results the studio wanted.

If NRG was in business in 1942, with Joe's help, Warner Brothers would have put Bogart on the plane with Ingrid Bergman, kind of ruining *Casablanca*.

There was not a single unique, surprising, or satisfying ending to a movie that could not have been ruined by Joe.

As we took our seats in the Challenger 604 jet, I turned to Joe but announced to the entire plane:

"You know Joe. I hate to fly. In fact, every time I get off a plane, I view it as a failed suicide attempt." This was prescient since three years later I would survive a Gulfstream II airplane crash at this very airport.

"The only good thing about getting on this plane with you, Joe, is the knowledge that if I die tonight in a plane crash, I'm taking you with me."

The entire plane, in unison, moaned "Baaaareeeeee," as if insulting Joe was going to affect our scores.

Before the rise of the internet and social media, before there was Rotten Tomatoes, all of which can ruin an unfinished movie's chances of success, film studios would have a series of recruited audience screenings with between 200 and 300 people. The studio and filmmakers would get information on how the movie played, where the audience might be confused, scenes where the laughs weren't playing, or when there was an increase in audience coughing and buttock shifting. Armed with this information, the director would return to the editing suite to try to make the film better.

Because social media is now what it is, studios are much more reticent about screening films in progress. They've cut way back in terms of frequency and size of screenings to avoid rumors about their unfinished films. Now the studios often rely on what are called "friends and family" screenings, which is what it sounds like. Unfortunately, 30 friends, family members, and agents aren't an accurate test of a movie's playability.

I've learned some things over the years of recruited screenings:

1. You can tell how a comedy is going to play in the first minute. There's always some joke that will get laughs at one

screening and not another. This is an indication of just how depressing the night will be.

2. Everything you're going to learn at one of these screenings is gleaned from being in the audience and listening to coughing. No questionnaires or focus groups are required. Being in the theater while your movie is playing tells you everything you need to know, which is basically, "make it shorter."

3. Some theaters are better for comedies than others. A more padded room with more sound deadening material is great for the soundtrack, but bad for comedies. An audience needs to hear themselves laugh. Paramount, in fact, built a second theater on their lot, and the first premiere to take place there was *Addams Family Values*. I tested the room that morning, called Sherry, and begged her to move the screening to their old theater, which was less sound perfect, but more bright and lively. Sherry refused. After the premiere she found me:
"I'm never screening a comedy in this room again!"

4. Keep the screening room cold. SONY's former chairperson Amy Pascal, who did four movies with me, wore her winter coat to my recruited audience screenings all summer long. Like David Letterman, I'm a big believer that cold is funny. The Ed Sullivan Theater, where Dave had his show, felt about 62 degrees. Screen a movie in a warm room, and you're dead. The audience falls asleep. Trust me.

My first run-in with Joe was at the recruited audience screening of *The Addams Family*. I had majored in Political Science so I knew how numbers could be manipulated. The way a question is worded can lead to a specific answer. In the case of that first *Addams Family*

Joe proclaimed we had too many "Very Goods" and not enough "Excellents."

"That's because audiences don't think of comedies as 'excellent.' In an audience's mind, 'excellent' means 'important,'" I explained.

"Not true," said Joe.

At our next screening I added two additional questions. He thought they were a waste of time, but did it to shut me up.

In addition to all the other lines of inquiry, such as:

How would you rate this movie?

Would you recommend it to a friend?

Who were your favorite characters?

Were you ever bored?

List your favorite scenes.

What are your feelings about the ending?

Did you like the music? [It was always temporary music, so a stupid question.]

To those inquiries I added:

Have you ever, in your life, seen a comedy you would rate as "excellent"?

And:

What was your favorite movie in the last three months?

ONE THIRD of the responders said they had *never in their lives* seen a comedy they would rate as "excellent."

Favorite movie of the last three months? Overwhelmingly, Billy Crystal's comedy *City Slickers*.

"That doesn't prove anything," was Joe's scientific response.

Studios think of themselves as businesses, but they are poorly run at best. No one can predict what movie will or won't succeed at the box office, but studio executives try to justify their decisions with anything that reeks of science or business, as opposed to:

"My gut tells me this is good."

A studio executive relying on their "gut" is a recipe for getting fired if you have a couple of duds in a row, although if you were a baseball player who got on base one out of three times at bat you'd be venerated in Cooperstown. The brilliant John Calley, who ran Warner Brothers, United Artists, and later SONY, was the exception. His gut was the best in the business.

The San Jose *Get Shorty* screening went well. The audience laughed in all the right places, and the numbers were good. Being in the audience, I found a few places where I needed to extend a shot because the audience was cutting off their laughter to hear the next line of dialogue. Always a good sign.

Then came the part of the evening designed to give the studio what it wanted and potentially crush my dreams. The specifics in this case was MGM's attempt to make me lose the scene where Ray Bones slaps a woman across her face. After the numbers were counted, the "focus group," a small audience sampling that is supposed to represent the larger group demographically, remained in the theater whereupon Joe Farrell asked the audience a series of questions, including:

"How did you feel about Ray Bones slapping the dry cleaner's wife in the face? Were all of you, show me hands, upset by the slap?"

Of course they were, Joe! That's the point of the scene. To *make* the audience afraid of Ray. They're supposed to be upset by the shocking slap.

The very, very, very little worthwhile information you can glean from a focus group is mined in the first three minutes. After that, it is just Joe Farrell masturbating. Fifteen minutes in, when the session had devolved into esoteric and banal complaints, I stood up and even though I had not raised my hand, asked a litany of particularly unimportant questions:

"What happens to the dry cleaner's wife?"

"What was General Motors thinking by putting only one sliding door on Chili's Oldsmobile Silhouette?"

"Did anyone think Danny DeVito was too tall to play the title role of 'Shorty'?"

"Alright asshole. You win," laughed Mike Marcus, MGM's chairman.

Grabbing the back of my jacket and pulling me down into my seat, Mike announced:

"We're done here, Joe."

Later that night we landed safely back in Van Nuys, with me once again surviving a suicide attempt. I was walking across the tarmac when Joe raced to catch up with me.

"Barry. Just so you know . . . which might help on future movies . . . my wife is a beautiful actress. You know, in case on your next one . . ."

"Good to know, Joe."

Commercials

There are many upsides to directing commercials. They have a short timeframe, pay well, and my name is not on the product, so good or bad it doesn't affect my career.

One of the easiest series of commercials was with Jerry Seinfeld for Acura, the sponsor of the first few years of his show *Comedians in Cars Getting Coffee*. Jerry came up with the concepts and scripts and I directed.

My favorite moment was during the black and white commercial parody of an old-time movie. We shot a couple of takes of a woman in an elegant evening gown with long white gloves holding down the power window button on an Acura MDX. After a couple of takes we were ready to move on when the account executive approached and whispered something in my ear.

"What does she want?" asked Jerry.

"She suggested the client would love a take where the actress presses the power window button briefly but doesn't leave her finger on the switch."

"Why?" Jerry asked.

"Well, we're selling one-press power windows, meaning you just press the button and the window goes down."

"Yeah?"

"And by keeping her finger on the switch, it doesn't sell the one touch thing."

"Tell them their version isn't funny," suggested Jerry.

I went over to the group of fearful execs huddled in the special "client" section of the stage delineated by a large rug, couches, several video monitors, and wicker baskets filled with off-brand airplane versions of chips and power bars.

"Jerry says it's not funny."

"Got it," they said in unison.

Many years ago I directed some commercials for Nike starring Jerry Rice, Troy Aikman, and Reggie White. After the shoot, I was heading to Dallas for Sweetie's parents' 50th wedding anniversary. Sweetie and I were recently married. I wanted to make a good impression with Beverly Ringo, Sweetie's mom, who loved the Dallas Cowboys. I brought my 8mm SONY video camera to the Aikman shoot and asked Troy to wish Tom and Beverly a happy 50th anniversary. Troy was great. I presented Tom and Beverly my gift: "Hi Tom. Hi Beverly. This is Troy Aikman of the Dallas Cowboys wishing you two a happy 50th wedding anniversary." I was welcomed into their family as if I weren't Jewish.

In a perfect world of commercials, you want a higher up either from the agency or the client side to be on your set. The more senior the executive, the more self-confident and the easier it is to punt the commercial as originally conceived and try something different. A year or two after the Aikman/Rice/White commercial I was lucky to have David Kennedy of Wieden+Kennedy on our shoot. Wieden+Kennedy was *the* creative agency of the day. The script called for a series of shots of a woman and dog out for a fast walk. The woman is wearing a new pair of Nikes and the dog's inner monologue is a complaint about how much faster and more often the owner walks in her new Nikes.

"Walk. Walk. Walk. All she does is walk."

I tossed out the shooting boards and asked David if he'd be OK with me attaching a leash to the camera hovering at ground level and use a shakicam as I did on *Raising Arizona* to scoot along the pavement. In effect, the camera is the dog's point of view. I'd follow close behind the new Nikes with the dog's voice-over complaining how much more walking they're doing since she bought her new Nikes. It worked great. If the founder of one of the most creative agencies in the world hadn't been on set that day, it's unlikely I would have been allowed to film the commercial in one continuous low angle shot. The other genius move was to put David in the commercial as an extra, which meant he couldn't sit around video village dissecting the shot.

I won a Clio—the equivalent of an Oscar in the world of commercials—one of three I received over the years. I was recently at a party where I met six-time Oscar nominated cinematographer Caleb Deschanel. What he most wanted to talk about was that Nike commercial.

One of the jobs of a commercial director is to entertain the clients and agency between setups.

I was directing a couple of UPS commercials for Ammirati Puris, a New York ad agency. There are only so many Will Smith, Tommy Lee Jones, Robin Williams, and John Travolta stories you can tell over the course of a shoot. During a particularly long lighting setup I proceeded to tell the assembled group about my apocalyptic nine-day career as cinematographer on nine feature length pornos. My horrific story ends with me covered in human excrement when a double insertion goes horribly wrong.

When I'm in the groove, I can stretch this story out to a good [or bad] half hour. My tale was well received, the DP was done lighting, and we went on with the commercial.

The next group of commercials the agency produced were directed by Kevin Smith. The team of executives told Kevin my porno story. I had no knowledge of this until months after his movie *Zack and Miri Make a Porno* was released theatrically. I received an email from Kevin confirming he stole my double insertion story, and how he'd love me to tell my version of the event on the director's commentary for the *Zack and Miri* DVD.

I passed.

The Single Most Asked Question of a Director

"**W**ill you see his shoes?" is the single most asked question of a director. Multiple times an hour.

Actors hate wearing their characters' shoes. If I could accumulate the time spent waiting for a wardrobe assistant to run back to some actor's trailer to fetch their shoes, I'd probably have enough banked time to film another movie. You might ask why doesn't the assistant wardrobe person arrive on stage with the actor's prop shoes *just in case* we might see the actor's feet? Or you could ask why doesn't the assistant ask the DP during the endless time the cinematographer is lighting if he'll see the actor's shoes? Or, you might wonder, why doesn't the dresser assigned to this actor just wander over to video village or any other monitor broadcasting the camera's live feed and take a gander at the stand-in who's standing on the actor's mark and see if there are feet in the frame. Sadly, this just never happens. Ever.

The other possibility is during lighting, you'll hear the voice of the wardrobe person over the assistant director's walkie-talkie squawk, "Joe, go to two," which means, go to channel two on the walkie-talkie so the entire crew, who are all on channel one, won't hear you ask about the shoes.

"Hey boss. Will we see his shoes?" the assistant director asks me.

Trying not to state the obvious in a passive aggressive way, you point to the monitor that is broadcasting the shot for all to see, and say, as if just discovering the answer, "Yeah, it looks like we do see his feet."

After more whispering on the walkie, the next question will be:

"Hey boss. Are we wide enough it doesn't matter what shoes he's wearing?"

Resisting the impulse to point to the monitor and go full-on silent schmuck, you calmly say, "Seems like he'll need his film shoes."

Here's what actually happens:

You're ready to roll camera and the script supervisor, who is in charge of continuity, announces: "Those aren't the proper shoes," at which point the assistant wardrobe person walks/runs to the actor's camper to fetch them.

The reason this shoe question is so prevalent is because actors' wardrobe shoes never seem to fit.

Some grizzled ol' timers have shoe hacks. One actor I worked with had his shoes sent to him as soon as we chose them. I think it was Hackman. He would wear his many pairs of prop shoes at home for half an hour a day, slowly breaking them in. This not only required wardrobe decisions to be made at least a month ahead of time, it also required a sign-off from various producers and studio heads, who have an almost fetishistic interest in wardrobe.

Tommy Lee Jones went one step further, requiring us to make shoe decisions even earlier. Tommy would have us send the shoes to his boot maker in Texas. Since Mr. Bootmaker had Tommy's foot form for his cowboy boots, he was able to make incredibly expensive identical looking shoes for Tommy's comfort.

Unfortunately, even with Tommy, the question was still asked before every setup:

"Will you see his shoes?"

Smoke and Mirrors

Agents K and J save the world. 1997.

I've always assumed there were aliens on Earth and Ed Solomon's script *Men in Black*, based on Lowell Cunningham's graphic novel, did a wonderful job creating a funny reality-based world in which they existed.

After Sweetie and I read Ed's draft, I called Walter Parkes and Laurie MacDonald, the *MIB* husband and wife producer team, and expressed interest. A few days later I flew out to Los Angeles where I met Walter, Laurie, Ed, and Lisa Henson, then president of production of Columbia Pictures, now SONY. This would be the first of dozens of in-person meetings, which meant constantly risking my life flying round trip from JFK to LAX.

Walter went to Yale, plays a mean guitar, and is handsome with a great head of silver hair. He is well read, articulate, and persuasive. He is married to Laurie MacDonald, a smart, pretty, charming woman. The two of them ooze Hollywood power couple. Lisa Henson is lovely—her father was Jim Henson, the puppeteer.

These meetings often took place in a large booth at the Broadway Deli, an imitation New York delicatessen, in Santa Monica. The pastrami, corned beef, and brisket sandwiches were minor league compared to Katz's. We would sit for hours listening to Walter lecture us on why the movie needed pheromones as the lynchpin for its plot.

"If I don't have pheromones, I have no movie," Walter would insist, very Scott Rudin–like. What was surely Walter's idea, the finale threatened the end of humanity due to the pheromones, or scents that humans give off when they're afraid. I'm simplifying, but in Walter's version, the voraciously hungry alien bugs are blind [I think] but are attracted to our scent of fear. Millions of these bugs, now on Earth, frighten all the humans. Our two hero Men in Black agents need to get everybody on Earth to laugh. Since no one is fearful, no one is exuding fear smells, and therefore the bugs can't smell anyone to eat. They perish. Mankind survives. If this sounds confusing, it's because it is. The script concluded with images of people all over the world, smiling, laughing, hugging. Cue "I'd Like to Buy the World a Coke." The end.

Really?

I could never move the needle off any idea Walter wanted to keep. Things got worse when Kathy Kennedy and Frank Marshall left Amblin Pictures and Steven Spielberg enlisted Walter and Laurie to be the new heads of his studio. Parkes/McDonald convinced SONY to let them bring *Men in Black* over to Amblin, which meant SONY would pay for and distribute the movie, but Spielberg would get a hefty percentage of the box office gross by allowing his name to be associated with this big budget film.

In a meeting with Walter, Laurie, Spielberg, and myself, Walter pitched Steven our ideas:

"Steven. Barry thinks the scene where K convinces J to join the Men in Black should happen like on a park bench or somewhere. Now here's my idea: It's sunset. The clouds part as the last rays of a spectrum of colors from a setting sun spread across the screen, the silhouette . . . "

"Hey. That's no fair," I whined. "I didn't get a sunset. I didn't get any rays of sun spreading . . . "

"Walter, give Barry some rays of sun," said Laurie.

Of course, Walter's presentation was brilliantly articulated. For Steven, it was an easy choice—go with the guy blessed with great hair and a beautiful sunset—although Steven added a weird twist suggesting J and K rub an alien gel on their hands that makes them laugh hysterically as they walk towards Walter's fucking spectrum of colors. After Spielberg left the meeting, I asked if we had to do the gel thing. The power couple dismissed the idea, promising that by tomorrow Steven would forget he suggested it.

I wanted to move the action from the scripted locations in Washington, DC, Las Vegas, and an underground alien bug lair in Lawrence, Kansas, to New York City, where I figured aliens would actually live. I figured aliens could "pass" in New York with very little disguise. I also kept unsuccessfully fighting Walter on the pheromones ending. It was an intellectual conceit, neither visual nor satisfying.

I left *Men in Black* when I finally got funding to make *Get Shorty*, a film I had been trying to direct for many years. I loved the concept of *MIB* but was eager to direct *Get Shorty*. I was also frustrated working with an intractable Walter. As I was told years later by a sage studio executive, "Walter Parkes can turn any green lit movie into a development deal."

I directed *Get Shorty* and was in postproduction when Sweetie and I were having Sunday brunch at the Ivy at the Shore in Santa Monica. I spotted Barry Josephson, Lisa Henson's replacement, sharing an egg white omelet with Uma Thurman.

In my absence from *Men in Black*, Walter, Spielberg, and SONY had hired Les Mayfield to direct. Les had two things going for him:

Word of mouth was that his remake of *Miracle on 34th Street* was going to be a huge hit. I also believe Les had directed a birthday video for Spielberg. I'm not sure if it was the disappointing box office of the remake, or perhaps the birthday video, but Mayfield was now off *MIB*. It could also be that Les couldn't come to grips with Walter's pheromones issue. After paying the bill for my gumbo yaya and crab cakes and Sweetie's grilled salad, washed down with Ivy gimlets, we stopped by Josephson's table.

"Sorry to interrupt, but if you guys are willing to wait for me to finish postproduction on *Get Shorty*, I'd love to come back and direct *Men in Black*. I think I could do a good job." I'm not sure how Walter felt about it, but SONY hired me back.

David Koepp came on to do a rewrite. He added mystery and manliness to what was already a good Ed Solomon script. He also got rid of the fucking pheromones.

I was at The St. Regis hotel in New York the night the fax machine that had been installed in my luxurious room started to dot matrix print the David Koepp rewrite. These pages would reveal if Koepp was able to make our mutual ideas work.

As each page slowly curled its way out of the fax machine, I was thrilled.

Except for one suspect scene, the pages were excellent. Suddenly the movie was something I could embrace and maybe make good.

"Hey Dave. Walter sent me your rewrite. It's funny and muscular. Just fantastic."

"Well thanks, Barry. I'm quite happy with it myself."

"One little thing: There's a scene I don't get, and I wonder why we need it."

"Read me the scene," Dave said.

I read it to him.

"I didn't write a word of it. It's awful. Walter must have written it and added it to my pages. Get rid of it."

Tender Lovin' Jones

"That's enough, Mikey. Put up your hands. *AND ALL YOUR FLIPPERS!*"

It's the first day of filming *Men in Black*. It took years to get here, but we are on Stage 27 at SONY's Culver City lot.

A week earlier I had scouted the stage with the camera, grip, electric, and visual effects crew which allowed Don Peterman, our director of photography, to get a jump on lighting this humongous set, designed to look like Arizona's Sonoran Desert. By building the dirt, cactuses, berms, hills, and even a road on stage, we could pre-light the set and film this night scene during the day. I asked our production designer, Bo Welch, for lots of cactuses since they have a certain comedic alien vibe.

We were carrying around a long stick with the head of "Mikey," an alien who Tommy Lee Jones interacts with in the scene. Rick Baker had designed the alien, a long-nosed creature with a body that included multiple flippers in addition to legs and arms. As we walked through the set, making sure everyone was prepared for our first day, we woke up a drunk electrician who had been sleeping in the rafters. Looking down from his perch 45 feet above the stage floor, a tad dismayed by the long-nosed alien head on a stick, he screamed in full drunk-person volume, *"SNORKELDORK!"*

And he wouldn't shut the fuck up about it.

"SNORKELDORK!" he'd cackle.

Mikey, aka "Snorkeldork," and his human disguise.

The inebriated electrician did nothing for our confidence. For the rest of my career working with Bo Welch, "Snorkeldork" became our synonym for "embarrassingly cheesy."

But it was now day one on *Men in Black* and I was about to direct the very intimidating Tommy Lee Jones. We had rehearsed and lit the scene and were ready for a profile master shot of Tommy Lee [Agent K], his soon to be retired partner [Agent D], and Mikey, who partway through the scene is revealed not to be an illegal alien from Mexico, but an illegal alien from another galaxy.

Mikey is in the middle of replying to Tommy's interrogation in his alien language, a puppeteer off camera controlling Mikey's mouth, eyes, and flippers using RC motors while another puppeteer wearing the Mikey costume controls his legs and arms.

Tommy interrupts Mikey and says:

"That's enough, Mikey. Put up your hands," at which point Mr. Jones sing-songs his way towards what he thinks should be a big time comedy punchline, *"AND . . . ALL YOUR FLIPPERS!"*

I broke out in an instant sweat. Until this shot, things had gone reasonably well. Yes, Tommy had fired his hair person, but truthfully, he inadvertently put her out of her misery. It would have been a daily torture for her to stay. Other than that, the first few shots had gone swimmingly. Tommy speaks fluent Spanish, which gave his dialogue with the van full of Mexican illegals a wonderful verisimilitude. But now it all came crashing down as I realized I was about to embark on a very, very, very long 20 weeks of directing an actor who was, gulp . . . *trying to be funny.*

"Cut. Good," I lied, as I walked towards Tender Lovin' Jones, staring at my script to avoid eye contact for as long as possible.

"Hey, Tommy," I said, still looking down at my script. "It will be funnier if you don't acknowledge that 'And all your flippers' is funny."

I looked up and found myself caught in Tommy's fiercely opinionated glare:

"See, Tommy, for you, this is all in a day's work. Very GI. Very Government Issue. Agent K doesn't think 'All your flippers' is funny. You're just saying it the same way you're saying, 'Put up your hands.' It's just normal police procedure. That's what makes it funny for the audience."

I brilliantly looked back down at my script so Tommy couldn't kill me with his laser focused eyes.

"Let's try one more!" I brightly called out. "It'll be fun!"

For 20 weeks, I wouldn't let Tommy be funny and for 20 weeks it was an extremely intimidating experience.

Tommy's agent, Michael Black, called.

"You don't want Tommy to be funny," Michael whined. "You only want Will Smith to get laughs."

"Not true, Michael. Think of any comedy duo. Abbott and Costello. George Burns and Gracie Allen. Dean Martin and Jerry Lewis. Lucy and Ricky Ricardo. You need one funny guy and one straight man but they both get laughs. In fact, I would argue the straight man gets the bigger laugh. The comedy is in the reaction shot."

"But, Barry."

"Michael. I promise. Tommy is as funny as Will. Trust me."

After Tommy saw the finished film and was asked at the *Men in Black* press junkets how he became so funny, Tommy's answer made up for five months of anxiety:

"Stand next to Will Smith and do whatever Barry Sonnenfeld tells you to do."

The Rancher and the Farter

When Sweetie and I first read *Men in Black*, I thought Tommy Lee Jones would be great as Agent K. Sweetie's suggestion was Will Smith as Agent J.

Spielberg and Walter and Laurie had pushed for Clint Eastwood as agent K and Chris O'Donnell for Agent J. I don't know what happened with Eastwood, but at a dinner at the Four Seasons hotel in LA that Spielberg requested I have with Chris O'Donnell, I convinced Chris I was a bad director, the script was never going to improve, and he should pass on *Men in Black*. Chris was an excellent actor—he was brilliant in *Men Don't Leave*—it was just that Sweetie wanted Will Smith for the part. Once Chris passed, I set up a meeting between Will and Steven at Spielberg's house in East Hampton, and the rest is history.

As soon as Tommy agreed to do the film, I took him to dinner at Röckenwagner, a continental restaurant in Santa Monica.

I had a plan.

Tommy had recently directed a television movie, *The Good Old Boys*, with my friend Fran McDormand. There is a scene where Fran is staring out the window, never looking back towards the man she's having a disagreement with.

"Tommy," I pretend-naively started: "In that scene with Fran staring out the window . . . It was such a specific choice, which I assume was yours, to not have Fran look at her husband. She plays the entire scene staring out the window."

"Yup."

"So, Tommy. What would you have done if Fran, or any actor, I guess, would have said, 'I wouldn't play the scene that way. I'd turn around'?"

"I would have articulated the reasons I didn't want her to turn around."

"And you think it's an actor's responsibility to do what the director tells them? I mean, even if they disagree?"

"Yes, Barry. I do."

I checked my imaginary tape recorder, making sure it recorded every word of Tommy's pronouncement, since I was sure I'd need it on the set.

Tommy didn't always agree with my direction, that's for sure, but he always did what I asked.

I was lucky Will started two weeks after filming began. This meant that, in effect, Will was joining, in progress, Tommy's movie. I was also lucky, and you never know until you start filming, that Mr. Smith and Mr. Jones had wonderful chemistry on and off the set. They each thought the other was hilarious.

You wouldn't expect this, but Tommy is like a hyperactive 6-year-old. Give him a prop and he will break it. Doug Harlocker, the prop master on all three *Men in Black* movies, begged me not to let Tommy hold the neuralyzer, a very intricate expensive prop, until right before my "action" call.

Every time he picked up one of the heavy MIB space weapons it was almost always when the assistant camera person was putting a tape mark on the ground. As the kid got on his knees, Tommy would heft the super heavy long space gun to his shoulder and there would be a horrible cracking sound as TLJ's gun contacted the assistant's chin.

"That boy better start paying more attention," Tommy declared.

Tommy holding one of the few neuralyzers he hadn't broken.

Over the course of three movies Tommy ruined many takes with his pretend gun sounds. Since all the weapons in *Men in Black* were space guns, any sounds they made were added in postproduction. Tommy, being a true cowboy [he prefers "rancher"], cannot abide a gun that makes no sound.

"And action," I would call out.

Tommy and Will would in unison lift their guns to shoot at a retreating Edgar and without fail, Tommy would pull the trigger of his Series IV de-atomizer while sound effecting an audible:

"Bjoing."

"Cut."

"*What?*" Tommy would jump on me.

"You did it again."

"No I didn't."

"Will?"

"Yeah, Tommy. You made the 'bjoing' sound again."

"No I didn't."

"OK! Let's try one more. It will be fun! And Tommy. No bjoinging."

I loved Tommy's performance. He is one of the few actors who can talk incredibly fast yet maintain perfect diction. His voice has a beautiful lilt—when not bjoinging.

It was a good thing Tommy liked Will, since Mr. Smith had a tendency to fart. The most horrific example took place on a blue screen stage in New York City. In the scene, Will and Tommy are driving upside down on the ceiling of the Midtown Tunnel. The physical effects team had built the interior of the Ford Galaxy, now transformed into a hypercar. This live element would be incorporated into the computer graphics car exterior.

Tommy and Will were locked in the shell, forklifted 15 feet in the air, and rotated. Now Tommy is harnessed to his seat upside down and Will is standing in effect on the interior windshield, since Agent J didn't put on his seatbelt. He is squatted down, inches from Tommy.

I rolled camera, put on my headphones, and heard Will Smith:

"Oh Jesus. Oh man."

"It's alright, Will," says a stoic Tommy.

"Hey Baz. Guys. Get us out of here. Get us down. We need a ladder. Hurry. Emergency! Get a ladder. Now!"

We race to flip the massive set, bring in a ladder, and pop the seals and locks that clamshelled the two halves together. As soon as the top opens, Tommy reaches his leg way out to meet the approaching rolling ladder and before it was even stabilized, Mr. Jones is on the ground, gasping for air.

Will had farted inside the hermetically sealed capsule and it was pretty ugly.

The Michael Bay Encyclical

The last weeks of shooting were on the New York World's Fair set built inside SONY's Stage 30. In the scene, Agents J and K must prevent Edgar Bug from leaving the planet or Earth will be destroyed.

After several rehearsals ratcheting Randy, Will Smith's stunt double, across the 31,000 square foot, 50-foot-high sound stage, Will whispered,

"Hey Baz. You want me to do it?"

Randy was a good stunt person, but having Will do the stunt would allow me to stay on his camera angle from the time he gives his line: "You just going to eat and run? What about dessert?" [the bug had just swallowed Tommy Lee Jones], through Edgar Bug brutally kicking Will high, wide, and out of frame. Without a cut, the audience would witness Will Smith himself doing this major stunt. Very cool.

The issue, and what made me hesitate [for a half second], is that this would be the biggest, most dangerous stunt I directed. We had a very good stunt crew who I trusted, so with just a nano-beat of hesitation, I said:

"Sure."

The prep for this shot was going to take a couple of hours, over-lapping lunch, so I headed to my camper, a place I rarely go.

A director never wants to be off set, except for lunch. Leave for an hour and return to discover the crew has ruined a cool low angle shot by raising the camera a foot since the low camera angle was seeing off the set and would have required the grips to spend a half hour putting in the ceiling

—*or conversely*—

the grip crew is putting in the ceiling piece because the camera is seeing off the set, and you wish someone would have asked, you would have told them to raise the camera a foot to save time.

Plus, the crew tends to work faster when the director is around.

I was in my camper racing through my tri-tip and mashed potatoes so I could take a nice long nap during the crew's lunch when there was a:

Powerful. Self-confident. Doom invoking knock on my trailer door.

"Come in," I screamed.

Standing outside a trailer, it is impossible to hear anyone inside yelling for you to enter. In fact, partway through filming, I had the teamsters put an intercom system inside and outside my camper so there could be a pre-entry discussion. Or at least I wouldn't have to scream every time someone knocked.

Will and Tron entered. They looked serious.

Tron had a baseball bat.

Tron was Will's first super-sized assistant. Quiet but deadly [like Will's farts]. He had the soft, kind face of an angel in training and a pear-shaped body the size of a manatee.

On later shows, Will's assistant was Charlie Mack, a Philly friend who would go on to seal the win for Obama in 2008, delivering Pennsylvania. Charlie distributed his massive weight differently than Tron, being much taller. Charlie had the voice of a subwoofer. Both Tron and Charlie were intimidating.

Me, I guess getting a massage, Will, and Tron. New York City.

Charlie Mack.

Here's what Will said:

"Hey Baz. Tron and I have decided to invoke the Michael Bay Encyclical."

"Michael Bay . . . "

"Encyclical. See, Baz. On *Bad Boys* a lot of guys were getting hurt."

"Michael was rushing things," said a soft-spoken Tron. "So Will came up with this rule."

"Encyclical," corrected Will. "I had Tron stand next to Michael and I explained to him that if something went wrong on a stunt, whatever injury to me, or any stunt person, Tron would inflict on Michael."

"Everything ran a lot safer after the encyclical," nodded Tron.

"So anyways, Baz. That's what we're invoking here: The Michael Bay Encyclical. I do the stunt. Tron stands next to you. If I'm good, you're good."

Will and Tron left the camper, but a nap was no longer in the cards.

Stage 30 was kept cold and wet to give the hundreds of pallets of sod a chance to survive a few more days. I was hoping my down jacket would soften the blows from Tron's bat, and prayed any damage to Will was not in the region of his head. Will and Tron were called to set. Will arrived and walked over to Mata, his dresser, to be harnessed and padded for his 100-foot rachet, sending him high into the air, hopefully landing in the hidden stunt pads on the other side of a berm we had created for this specific angle.

Tron split from Will and walked towards me, giving a reassuring grin while simultaneously tapping his baseball bat.

"Good luck, Baz," Tron smiled.

"Yup. Thanks.

"Roll camera . . . "

"Hey. Whereya going?" Will yells towards the yellow tennis ball eye-line, placed near the crane mounted camera, eventually to be replaced by a computer graphics Edgar Bug. "You going to eat and run, huh? What about desserrrrrr . . ."

At which point Will is violently yanked, mid-word, high and wide and out of frame.

"Cut!" I scream.

"Will? How am I?"

"You're good, Baz."

"Congratulations, Baz," nods Tron, as he slings his bat over his shoulder, lumbering towards Will to help him climb out of the stunt pads.

Will being yanked out of frame. CGI Edgar Bug in foreground.

Losing Lincoln Center

Bo and I were devastated when we lost Lincoln Center as the location for Will Smith's first alien encounter. The plan was for Will, a New York City cop, to chase the alien across the Lincoln Center Plaza, into the Metropolitan Opera House, and up to its roof where the alien would jump to its death. At the last minute, Lincoln Center changed its mind and we had no location.

Bo came into my office with a photography book and a grin on his face.

"How could we not have thought of this in the first place?" he asked as he put the open book on my desk.

"It's kinda better than Lincoln Center," I replied. "Is it available? Will they give us the interior? And the roof?"

"Locations is pretty sure we can have it all."

A few hours later our minivan pulled up to the Guggenheim Museum. Bo and I had tried to put lots of circles in the movie. Nothing says flying saucers better than circular objects, and few buildings in New York City were rounder than the Guggenheim. With a few rules to protect their art, the museum agreed to participate.

Designed by Frank Lloyd Wright, the building was controversial when it opened in 1959. A lot of the complaints were about its shape, which didn't conform to other buildings in the neighborhood, in that it was *round*.

"The Perp" running towards the Guggenheim Museum.

Sweetie is a big believer in kismet. When we lose an actor, for instance, she promises we'll find someone better. My personal philosophy is "there's no upside to optimism," so we differ in that way. We were passed over by a lot of actors before Chris Lloyd agreed to be Fester. I can't imagine anyone better than Neil Patrick Harris as Count Olaf in Netflix's *A Series of Unfortunate Events*, though he was not the studio's first choice. Dustin Hoffman, Warren Beatty, and many others passed on playing Chili Palmer before we landed Travolta.

We lost Lincoln Center and ended up with something better.

I hate heights, so filming on the roof of the Guggenheim was difficult. I had cast Keith Campbell, a stuntman and now an actor, to play the alien perp. I intended to film Keith in a continuous shot as he backed up to the edge before back flipping off the Guggenheim roof to the pavement a hundred feet below. Keith started out life as a national gymnastics champion and in fact doubled Raul Julia doing a triple backward summersault, landing in Gomez's chair in *The Addams Family*.

Earlier that afternoon, the stunt crew rehearsed this perilous feat using a device called a decelerator. They weighed Keith and grouped together a bunch of sandbags of equivalent heft. The plan was to test the system without using a presently living Keith. The stunt team tied one end of a cable to the sandbags, while the other end snaked its way to the top of the Blakley Tree Service crane, 50 feet above us. The cable then stretched down to the street below where it was attached to the decelerator. A decelerator is a huge cylinder, shaped like an ice cream cone lying horizontally, that has huge fan blades sticking out of it.

The concept, and believe me, this seemed like a really dumb idea at the time, was that Keith would step off the edge of the building and do a backward layout as he free-fell towards Fifth Avenue, his back parallel to the ground, his face and stomach facing me and the heavens above. As Keith fell towards what I assumed, if I was doing it, certain death, the slack in the cable, which had been clipped to the harness under his clothes, tightened and started to slowly spin the fan blade. The nearer Keith got to terra-very-firma, the tighter the pull on the cable, the faster the fan blade spun. The faster it spun, the more wind resistance, slowing Keith from full stupidity to a dead stop ten feet before impact when I cut back to Will Smith looking on in disbelief.

It was a perfect night for filming. It was warm and we seemed to own New York, with movie lights and equipment at different locations. We started the night with Keith jumping off the 32nd Street Park Avenue overpass where decades earlier I had enjoyed Chock Full o'Nuts heavenly coffee every morning while waiting for the Network Couriers vans to arrive for my 6 to 9 AM gig delivering packages. Along with my summer job as the relief elevator operator at 40 Wall Street, Network Couriers helped me stay afloat financially while attending film school.

Back at Park Avenue, the gag was for Will's character, a New York City cop, to jump off the overpass and land on top of an open-air tour bus where he ad-libbed to a gaggle of Japanese tourists the brilliant: "It just be raining Black people in New York." Keith did the jump, Will overlapped the landing.

We then moved to Fifth Avenue and 89th where we filmed the first part of the scene where Will tracks down Keith just outside Central Park, across the street from the Guggenheim.

Another great ad-lib from Will in this scene was:

"**NYPD**. Which means I will k**N**ock **Y**our **P**unk **A**ss **D**own."

It took me a few years to realize that Knock starts with a silent K and not an N, but good one, Will!

Keith had Will press hard against his back and used a combination of that pressure and the Central Park wall in front of him to do a 180 degree backflip before racing across Fifth Avenue at which point, using a cable and the Blakley crane, he scaled the side of the Guggenheim Museum.

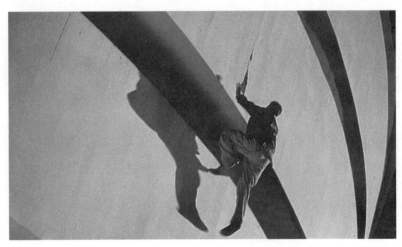

With the help of postproduction cable removal, Keith scales the Guggenheim.

Already a great night and the best was yet to come.

The decelerator tests earlier in the day went well, and we were now ready to film our terrifying stunt with Keith, not sandbags.

"Are you nervous?" I asked Keith.

"Are you kidding? Of course I'm nervous."

"I mean, I can't blame you. How many times have you done a stunt with a decelerator?"

"Never."

"You've never jumped off a building before?"

"Nope."

"Jeez. No wonder you're scared."

"Oh. Sorry. Misunderstanding. I'm not scared about the stunt. I'm scared about acting in a dialogue scene with Will Fucking Smith."

"So the jump?"

"Piece of cake."

And it was.

Keith, having gotten through the nerve-wracking acting part of the scene, pancaking his way towards the sidewalk below. Please note the circles [flying saucers?] on the sidewalk. Credit goes to Frank Lloyd Wright.

Rip Torn

I first became aware of Rip Torn at film school when my directing class screened *Coming Apart*, a 1969 film directed by Milton Moses Ginsberg. Rip played a mentally unstable psychiatrist who secretly filmed sexual exploits with his patients.

The irony of a movie called *Coming Apart* starring *Rip Torn* was overlooked by my NYU directing professor who believed the best movie ever made was *The Sound of Music*.

There was a particularly disturbing scene involving Sally Kirkland, an open chest of drawers in which sat a duck, and Rip. If I remember correctly, the plan was for Rip to stick his penis in the duck's mouth at which point Sally would slam the drawer shut. My memory could serve me wrong.

I mean, I hope it does.

Tommy Lee Jones and Rip Torn are both Texans.

They hated each other.

Rip played Zed, the guy in charge of Men in Black. Tommy played Agent K, its top agent. Tommy was the rancher/shotgun kind of Texan. Rip was the make your own lures for trout fishing kind of Lone Star citizen.

Rip was an angrier Texan than Tommy, which is saying *a lot*.

Early in the film, Tommy [Agent K] is showing newly recruited Will Smith [Agent J] MIB Headquarters, designed by Bo to resemble the Eero Saarinen TWA [now JetBlue] terminal at JFK.

Both Zed and Agent K are manly men of few words who have seen everything, not unlike Rip and Tommy.

After being introduced to Zed, as J and K are walking away, Zed calls out:

"K. Give the kid some fire power."

That's what was written.

Given Rip's Texas accent, what Zed yelled out was:

"K. Give the kid some far par."

"Cut."

"Hey, Rip. Can you say 'Fire. Power.'"

"That's what I said."

"OK. Well, really, um, enunciate 'Fire. Power.' And . . . Action!"

"Hey, K. Give the kid some Far Par."

"Cut."

"What?!" Rip bellowed.

"Hey, Rip: FI-YER-POW-ER."

"That's what I've been fucking saying, God damnit."

"*Riiiight.* Well, um, let's try just one more."

"Hey, K. Give the kid some Far Par."

What I didn't know was after each take, Tommy complained to Will about what a fucking idiot Rip was. Will thought it was hilarious.

As I was saying, "So, Rip. Let's try 'Hey, K. Give the kid a weapon,'" Tommy was saying to Will, "Can someone tell that poor bastard to say, 'Give the kid a gun?'"

As was true for all three *Men in Black* movies, the script for our first one was constantly in flux. We were literally ad-libbing a series of totally different endings to the plot in real time. Not the way to make a 93 million dollar film.

We found ourselves debating, *on the set*, after 3 years of development, 4 months of preproduction, and 18 weeks of filming, the pluses and minuses of two different endings:

Number one being that Earth happened to be located between two warring planets and we're just collateral damage—"the rock that a cowboy hides behind"—as Walter Parkes was fond of saying.

Or:

The war between the two feuding worlds was required to take place in an area devoid of intelligent life, and that was Earth. Neither version was particularly satisfying since in both cases, earth and the Men in Black were passive participants.

After a lot of on-set debate between Will, Tommy, and me, we decided on the "devoid of intelligent life" version, a line Rip was going to have to deliver.

Rip was fuming in his trailer, his sad toupee sitting next to a bunch of monofilament, hooks, and feathers. He liked to blow off steam by making his own fishing lures.

To each his own.

"So Rip. Sorry for the delay. We feel the best version is for you to tell Will that our world is going to be destroyed because the battle between the two alien planets has to take place at a location devoid of intelligent life, and that's Earth."

"Of course that's what you guys picked. Of course you would pick a sentence with the word 'devoid' in it. I bet Tommy was all over *that* idea. Easy for him to say, since he's not the one who actually has to say 'devoid.' Let's give *him* a sentence with 'devoid' in it and see how *he* likes it. Devoid!"

"Hey, Rip. Is there a problem with 'devoid'? I mean, you just said it like half a dozen times.

"Problem? Problem? Why would there be a problem? Tommy Fucking Lee Fucking Jones."

"OK then. Great. See ya on set."

Rip Torn, agent Zed, at MIB Headquarters.

Sugar Water

A helpful habit I learned from Scott Rudin while directing the two *Addams Family* movies was to re-read the script and look at the assembled footage every Sunday. As filming progresses you discover things about your movie: Leaps in logic you thought would need explanation make perfect sense; every scene starts with the same camera move; a not yet photographed scene feels unnecessary; you realize there are five scenes in a row in a car; your close-ups are too tight; there isn't enough action. And in the case of *Men in Black, WE HAD NO ENDING.*

Because I read the *Men in Black* script every Sunday, on Monday I would call Walter, Laurie, and Lucy Fisher, SONY's vice-chairperson [there was no chairman after the departure of Mark Canton and the John Calley/Amy Pascal team had not yet come aboard] to ask if they had re-read the script. No? Well, here's some news: We have no ending. We also have an action-adventure comedy with almost no action.

Our film's climax consisted of Will Smith debating the nature of the universe with a million dollar, 15-foot-tall animatronic Rick Baker designed Edgar Bug.

A debate.

The huge puppet could bend up and down and articulate its mouth and arms, and looked really cool, but it could not move.

It was locked to the ground, which is what our unfortunate script called for.

With only a couple of weeks of filming left, I begged my partners to please, this weekend, read the script. We need a writer. We need an ending with some action. The Monday morning that started week 17 I got a call from Lucy, Laurie, and Walter. They had re-read the script and agreed our ending sucked. With only a couple of weeks left to write, prep, and shoot a new ending, the only writer who seemed to be available was one of the writers formerly of *Friends*. He scripted a few gags, but no action.

"We need to lose the debate," I kept whining. "We need Edgar in motion, climbing up the tower to his flying saucer and we need Will fighting Edgar, trying to keep him on the planet. When that fails, we need Will to do something that makes Edgar turn around and climb back down from the tower."

I offered two suggestions: The first was to put an old rotting dumpster with hundreds of cockroaches on the World's Fair set. Will is violently tossed off Edgar Bug's body as Edgar is climbing the tower, hits the dumpster hard, and roaches start scattering. Will starts stepping on Edgar's relatives, forcing Edgar to make his way back down the tower to protect his kin.

My second suggestion was, since it's established Edgar likes sugar water, we could have an old Coke machine that Will is thrown against instead of the dumpster. Will shoots the vending machine, spilling sugar flavored soft drink onto the ground. Edgar can't resist and makes his way off the tower to drink some soda and confront Will. We ran both suggestions by Spielberg. He preferred the roaches. Will ad-libbed most of the scene.

What I didn't expect was the requirement to have an officer of the ASPCA on set to protect the roaches. After each take, the roach wrangler, not to be confused with the ASPCA guy, had to count the little critters and find any missing ones before we were allowed to do another take. I asked the ASPCA guy if roaches really needed protection, and he had a good response:

"Where do you draw the line?"

"Excuse me?"

"If we don't protect roaches, do we not protect spiders? Caterpillars? Snakes? And then what? Pretty soon you're asking for a waiver for horses, dogs, cats . . . "

"Well, I'm not sure we should protect cats."

"Is that supposed to be funny?"

What seemed counterintuitive about the whole ASPCA thing was that when we were done filming, the ASPCA roach protection guy had no problem letting us fumigate the stage.

In addition to needing money for this new, action-packed-ish ending, I needed funds for an opening credit sequence. I had storyboarded [with Alan Munro, *The Addams Family* visual effects supervisor] a cool opening to our film, tracking a dragonfly that ends the opening credit sequence by flying into the windshield of the van carrying the illegal aliens, but there was no money for it.

I also felt we needed the film to have a great last shot—a shot that visually epitomized the theme of our entire movie, which is: *We don't have a clue.*

I wanted money to create a live action/CGI hybrid shot showing the relative scale of the infinitesimally small Earth compared to the almost limitless cosmos.

My plan was to start with a live action helicopter shot showing Will Smith and his new partner, the morgue attendant Linda Fiorentino, getting into their car. Zoom back as far as we can with a helicopter and zoom lens, then transition to a computer graphics image that seamlessly continues to pull back as it widens out from Manhattan Island, past the US, past Earth, past our solar system and galaxy for light years, finally revealing that our universe is inside a marble, and we are merely part of an alien child's game. It was the essence of our film.

I asked Walter to have Spielberg talk to SONY on our behalf. We needed a total of one and a half million dollars for the new opening and closing sequences, plus three million for the action-packed CGI revamped World's Fair Edgar scene.

"I'm not going to ask Steven," Walter bravely stated.

"Don't you want to make the movie better?"

"I'm not asking Steven."

"OK, Walter. *You* ask SONY."

"Not my job."

"*Not your job?!*"

"Steven will feel asking the studio for that kind of money is irresponsible and I'm his partner, so I won't ask the studio either."

"You're also *my* partner, Walter. In fact, your main job as producer is to hire the right director, which you've done, and then do whatever you can to help that director make the best movie possible. The worst that happens is you ask for the money and the studio says no. I mean, it's not like it's your money."

"Ask if *you* want, Barry, but neither Steven nor I will go to the studio for that kind of money."

So, I asked.

It was an embarrassing moment for both Lucy Fisher and me, which we still laugh about. Lucy entered my trailer and sat next to me on the couch.

My mother had great "strength through weakness." In her case, that usually meant threatening suicide.

In my case, I cried.

As Lucy Fisher sat next to me, I started to weep. Then I put my head on her lap.

"What's wrong," she asked, while surely being slightly creeped out.

"I need four and a half million dollars to finish the film in a good way."

"Wow. That's a lot," she gulped.

I talked Lucy through the scenes. She approved the money on the spot. Lucy *really* wanted out of there, even if it cost her studio millions.

How Last-Minute Subtitles Saved *MIB*

At some point during postproduction on *Men in Black*, John Calley replaced Mark Canton as SONY's chairman. A year earlier, Mark had refused to green light *Men in Black* because he didn't want to tell his SONY bosses in Japan the budget was 93 million. He suggested I sign an 84 million dollar budget, with a secret understanding between us I would go 9 million over budget.

"Look, Barry. We both know I can't green light a 93 million dollar budget."

"So we're not making the movie?"

"We're making the movie. Just not for 93 million."

"Right. But that's what it costs."

"Except if the Japanese find out I approved a 93 million dollar film they'll fire me."

"So we're *not* making the movie."

"I just told you we're making the movie! For 84 million."

"I can't make it for 84."

"No one's asking you to."

"I'm confused."

"The movie is officially 84 million. The Japanese will be happy, and you get to make your movie. You'll just go 9 million over budget."

"That will ruin my reputation as a director and put insane pressure on me."

"Well, Barry. I can't green light 93."

"So you're, and I think I keep saying this, not making the film."

"Are you not listening to me? Are you stupid? You're making the movie. I'm just not green lighting it."

"And the budget is . . . ?"

"Don't tell me. Just go make the fucking movie. And Barry. I. Did. Not. Green. Light. It."

Earlier in his career, when he was running Warner Brothers, Canton was the guy who threatened my former agent, Jim Berkus, that if I didn't give up *Forrest Gump*, I'd never work in this business again.

Anyway, Canton was no longer with SONY. John Calley, along with his new second in command, Amy Pascal, and the rest of us had attended a recruited audience screening [run, of course, by the antichrist Joe Farrell] the previous night. The next morning we were in a conference room in SONY's Thalberg Building assessing how we could, with very little time before our July 4 opening weekend, make the movie's plot easier to follow.

"I wish the plot was just a little easier to follow and had bigger stakes," said Calley. "The fact that there are two warring planets, neither of which is us but the war has to be on Earth because we're devoid of intelligence? It seems unsatisfying."

"There's a way to change the plot to make it more visceral," I realized. "And it won't require any additional shooting."

"How is that possible?" Walter demanded.

"There's only one scene that sets up the plot: two feuding planets will go to war if one of the planets doesn't give the other one 'Orion's Belt,' which as we know, Mike Nussbaum's planet is hiding here on Earth. That's the scene at Leshko's diner between Mike

Nussbaum and Carel Struycken playing the ambassadors of the two enemy planets. What if we get a linguist to watch the scene and create an alien language that we can ADR into Mike and Carel's mouths. Then we subtitle the alien dialogue into English and make the scene not about feuding planets, but instead, the two actors are from the *same* planet. Carel is warning Mike that Edgar Bug has come to Earth and is seeking Orion's Belt and to be careful because if Edgar gets Orion's Belt, it's bad news for every planet throughout the galaxy. Before our ambassadors can act on the warning, Edgar Bug kills both of them and starts tracking down Orion's Belt.

"The rest of the plot is now easier to follow [although nothing about this plot is particularly easy]. The good alien planet, the protector of Orion's Belt, with their ambassadors dead, wants the Men in Black to find and deliver it to them or they'll have to destroy Earth [and Orion's Belt] rather than let Edgar Bug have it. The big board at MIB Headquarters can show the dead ambassadors' attack ship waiting to blow up Earth."

"Too simple," says Walter.

"I like it," counters John Calley.

"We can have another screening with changes in a week," I offered.

Everyone loved the idea except Walter, who thought we were dumbing down the movie. The rest of us thought we were making it comprehensible and exciting.

A week later we screened the new version and the top two boxes [Excellent and Very Good] of the recruited audience questionnaires were up a substantial amount. We had been at 78 and went up to 89, a very respectable number that made everyone happy.

Except Walter.

Men in Black became, at that point, the highest grossing film in SONY's history.

The Problem with Aliens

I'm very fond of seven time Academy Award winner Rick Baker. He designed the aliens for all three *Men in Black* movies, as well as a creepy, funny looking artificial ear that mimicked RCA Victor's "his master's voice" gramophone speaker for *Wild Wild West's* Bloodbath McGrath.

Rick taught me to use puppets or actors in alien suits and makeup, rather than computer graphics, whenever possible. Puppeteers are actors. They can interact with your cast, respond to ad-libs, and even ad-lib themselves. The worm guys in the first *Men in Black* were "rod puppets." We placed the worms in the coffee break room on cabinets and near walls so rods sticking though the wall could control the puppets via the puppeteers hidden behind the set. The worm guys' bodies hid the rods from the camera's lens. I was able to change dialogue in real time and equally important, the scene was complete when we were done filming for the day with no need for special effects.

After the first take in the coffee break room I told Tommy to ask a worm guy if the coffee he was pouring was decaf, and I had the puppeteer respond, "Viennese Cinnamon," on the spot. I loved those worm guy puppeteers. The challenge with this approach is the director has to make decisions ahead of time, down to the precise camera height, the lens selection, and the exact location of the camera so the holes in the walls can be drilled and the puppets placed ahead of time. Not a problem for a preproduction nut like me.

Rod puppet serving "Viennese Cinnamon" coffee. All live action. No VFX.

By *Men in Black 3*, I told Rick I wanted to create unique aliens. We looked at a lot of undersea creatures for alien designs and then I went a step further.

"Every alien we've had so far is based on our human biases. They have legs and arms and mouths and eyes and noses. Let's try some non-human biased aliens."

Rick took up the challenge and a few weeks later presented some options.

"These are great, Rick. Just a few questions."

"Shoot."

"If they have no eyes, how does the audience know where the alien is looking, or what it's looking at."

"OK. We'll give it eyes."

"And without a mouth how do we know if it's thinking or talking."

"So you want a mouth?"

"I think we'd better."

"Got it."

"And don't we need arms or some kind of appendage for them to hold a weapon?"

By the end of the discussion we were back where we always were. Eyes, mouths, arms, legs.

We did have one alien in the kitchen of Wu's Chinese restaurant that was an exact duplicate of a real fish, so our discussions at least as it related to undersea creatures, wasn't totally for naught.

Rick Baker created "Bob" fish and
Will Smith hamming it up.

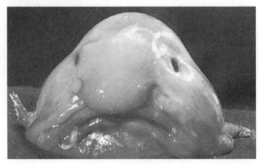

Real Blobfish.

Why Are We Here Mel? Part 1

Mel Bourne was the production designer on many Woody Allen movies. On several of those films, the brilliant Gordon Willis was the director of photography. In most cases the production designer is on a show a month or two before the cinematographer and has already started location scouting. I heard from Mel's son, Tim, who was the production manager on *Big*, that once Willis and Mel were both on salary, their van would pull up to a previously approved-by-Mel location, everyone would pile out and wait with fear and trepidation to hear from Gordon, who could be quite intimidating.

"Why are we here Mel?" meant Gordon didn't like the location and everyone would silently slink back into the van.

"Why are we here Mel?" became Bo's and my nickname for horrible locations.

Location scouting is possibly my least favorite part of filmmaking. I used to joke with Bo that a perfect location manager would be so bad that we'd have to build everything on stage, which I much preferred.

Rob Striem, the location manager on *MIB3*, made location scouting almost bearable. He had an amazing knowledge of the best restaurants in New York and would arrange our scout to make sure we were eating lunch at a certain time, in a certain borough, so we could order the best Chinese food in Manhattan. Or Queens.

I'm always in the front passenger seat of the van. As soon as I meet the driver, I wave my arm across the dashboard and announce, "From here to there [PRNDL to driver's window] is yours, and from here to there, I'm in control," which meant I was responsible for HVAC and the radio.

In addition to the driver and me, there's the production designer, locations team, sometimes the first assistant director, and perhaps the production manager. Eventually the cinematographer, once hired, will join in on the tedium. In the back of the van are multiple coolers with drinks and snacks.

Upon getting in the van, we're handed the menu for that day's lunch. We fill out our choices and the locations assistant calls in the order and time of arrival to the restaurant. Very efficient unless I ask for a list of the day's specials. That can slow things down.

After a couple of months of locking down locations, and close to the start of principle photography, we spend several days on the "tech scout," scouting with the department heads and their seconds—often the first time the crew has seen the locations. This bigger scout is either in a bus or multiple vans.

One of the highlights on *MIB3*'s endless scouts was our embarrassingly extravagant lunch at Peter Luger in Brooklyn. We started with my suggestion of a bunch of hamburgers "for the table." Then shrimp cocktails for everyone. We each ordered a NY strip or rib eye, plus the requisite family sized creamed spinach and several potato options. Not yet sated, we finished off lunch with shared key lime pie, plus cheese, chocolate, and carrot cake [no raisins]. Pretty much all of us, except our driver, had multiple martinis. No surprise, we slept in the van from Brooklyn to Jones Beach where we scouted what would become the launch pad for Cape Canaveral.

A Wild Mistake

After the success of *Men in Black*, I signed a movie production deal at Disney, followed by a lucrative television deal at SONY. I was happy. I should have known better.

Will and I looked for another project to do together.

James Lassiter, Will's business partner and producer, sent me *Wild Wild West*. I loved the mid-'60s television series, which combined westerns with science fiction. After a long negotiation, a series of additional writers, a surreal meeting with producer Jon Peters, and a death threat from Robert Conrad [the star of the original television show], we were ready to go.

At some point late in preproduction, I received a call from Robert Conrad. He wanted to have lunch.

We met at the Hotel Bel-Air. Near the end of a tense, contentious meal, as I was picking up the tab, Conrad leaned over and in a gruff whisper threatened:

"It's quite simple, Barry. My mob friends in Detroit don't want to see a Black boy play James West so you and your actor guy better figure out what you're going to do about that little problem, because someone is going to get hurt. Or worse."

I called James Lassiter.

"I just had lunch with Robert Conrad. He says he has mob friends in Detroit that will kill us if Will plays James West. He says his guys in Detroit don't want to see a Black guy playing a role he created."

"Detroit? Detroit? He's threatening us with mobsters from Detroit? Give me a break. We're from Philly. Let it go, Baz. We're all good here."

So I let it go. And I guess Detroit let it go too.

Until Thanksgiving morning, 1997, I thought the movie was going to star Will Smith and George Clooney. George had come out to the Hamptons a couple of months earlier and spent a weekend at our Amagansett home. My producing partner, Barry Josephson, joined us. George, no surprise, is a charming, funny guy.

Our weekend started slightly off kilter when George, Sweetie, and the Barrys had lunch at the Maidstone Arms, a venerable East Hampton eatery. The staff was so aflutter they created a special dessert: sugar cookies in the shape of bats—in homage to George's recently released *Batman & Robin.*

"Is this some kind of joke?" George asked our fresh-faced Irish waitress. [George was not happy with the film.]

"Sorry, sir. We wanted to . . . "

"Well, it's not funny."

After I paid the bill and smiled at the deflated staff, the four of us got into my 1962 white Lincoln Continental convertible—not unlike the one JFK was riding in when shot in Dallas. I had previously owned two but sold one to MC Hammer while directing *The Addams Family.*

We were tooling down Main Street when George caught a glint of sun reflecting off a paparazzi's telephoto lens, or maybe a rifle scope, or probably neither of those things. In any case, thrown off his game by the bat-cookies, George pulled a Jackie Kennedy and tried to climb over the trunk and out the back of the car. I think it was a joke.

Our new writing team, Jeff Price and Peter Seaman, worked on a new draft of the script, solving some but not all our story problems. The stench in the room was Jon Peter's insistence that there must be a scene where Will Smith appears in drag. As horrible as that sounds, it got worse. On Thanksgiving morning, Clooney called. He didn't like the new draft. Will had more funny lines than George. He was bailing.

We needed a new co-star.

We mistakenly hired Kevin Kline.

Kevin is a lovely, talented guy but took our film for the wrong reason—checking only one of the three powerpoint boxes for taking a movie: money. He was paid more than he had ever earned but had no love for the project and felt he was slumming. If you can't check off at least two out of the three boxes—pass.

Then there was Kevin's other issue:

Kenneth Branagh.

Both actors thought they were the greatest living Shakespearean actor. Or at least Kline did. It was a rare day when Kevin, knowing Branagh was already on set, didn't arrive pontificating, "A rose by any other name . . . "

Some scenes in the third act were shot on a set built on top of a gimballed platform placed in front of blue screen. In postproduction, these shots would be integrated into the computer graphics gigantic spider. Our first day of filming on this massive platform, with pistons, gears, and hydraulics, Kevin showed up on set after Will and Kenneth had already arrived.

"A rose by any other name . . . "

Oh, Jesus.

"So, Baz," Kline asked, "how many feet off the ground are we pretending this thing is?"

"Forty."

Barry Sonnenfeld

"Really? Not sixty?"

"OK. Sixty."

"Interesting. Is it forty or sixty?"

"How will that affect your acting, Kevin?"

"Well, I'm curious. First you say forty, then sixty . . . "

"It's forty."

"Back to forty?"

"Don't engage!" shouted Will.

There are scenes in *Wild Wild West* I really like. Will and Kevin's meet and greet at Fat Can Candy's bar and whore house had both comedy and well-choreographed stunts. Many scenes shot on the train, including using a man's head as a projector lens, were also fun. As always, Bo did a brilliant job designing the sets.

Unfortunately, there was zero chemistry between our two leads.

Kevin, cast as the straight man, couldn't help himself. He needed to be "funny."

Not the plan.

After the third day of filming, I took Will aside:

"You thinking what I'm thinking, Will?"

"You mean, am I thinking I have to be the straight man, since we don't want two funny people in our comedy and we'll never get Kevin to be the 'not funny' one?"

"Exactly."

As unfortunate as Will Smith playing the straight man in a comedy was, the third act was saddled with the very embarrassing Will Smith female impersonator strip tease Jon Peters had insisted on. It was truly horrible.

"If I don't have Will Smith in drag, I have no movie," I can imagine Peters screaming to Bob Daly and Terry Semel, Warner Brothers co-chairs.

198

Not a pretty picture. Will Smith in drag.

I was often unpolitical, short tempered, and in general a bad egg in my relations with the studio. I was angry I couldn't get rid of Jon Peters, angry I was spending millions of dollars on a huge set for a bad Will Smith in drag scene, and furious I was in a position of responsibility but had to defer to Peters on the script. Coming off the successes of *Addams Family Values*, *Get Shorty*, and *Men in Black*, I was deeply depressed I was working on a bad movie I didn't know how to fix.

Jon Peters is complicated. He wants to be loved but his go-to reset is that of a bully. He also, on occasion, made unfortunate clothing decisions. He once arrived at Sweetie's and my rental house on Foothill Road in Beverly Hills costumed in a neon yellow dong-sling and shearling-lined caveman vest, and nothing else. He had come to yell at me about something.

"Why did Crazy Jon come to our house in his panties?" asked a confused 4-year-old Chloe.

I've seen him, when angry, literally foam at the mouth.

Wild Wild West, along with my next film, *Men in Black II*, were the two most disappointing movies I directed. My career in Hollywood never recovered.

Jon Peters, space invader. My broken hand will be explained later.

The First Time

Movie sets are usually boring. The ratio of time spent with film running through the camera versus setting up for and lighting a shot is, if you're lucky, ten to one.

Over the course of several tedious days in one specific train car, due to lighting the cramped set and resetting various physical effects [a flipping pool table was one of them], Will and I were so bored we played the following game: Who could punch the other guy's shoulder harder.

This was of course, very dumb.

I would punch Will's shoulder as hard as I could and he would howl with laughter. Will would punch my upper arm and now it was my turn to howl, crumpling to the ground in agony, which also made Will howl with laughter.

Will only plays to win. He won't play half-speed. I received no slack for being physically weak, good-natured, or the director.

After a couple of days of torture, I decided enough is enough:

I am going to hurt this man.

I conjured up all the rage I could muster, shot my arm towards the fucker's massive shoulder with all the semi-manly force I was capable of, and immediately collapsed to the ground in excruciating pain. Will Smith's shoulder had broken my fifth metacarpal in five places.

After Will stopped laughing, he offered his hand to my remaining good one. I stood up and walked to the Warner Brothers medical offices, located on the studio lot.

"And what happened here?" asked the doctor.

I couldn't say I broke my hand hitting our lead actor. We were going to need an insurance day since I was in no shape to go back and direct, and a day on *Wild Wild West* cost a quarter of a million dollars.

"Someone, I'm not sure who, opened the stage door on my hand."

"Opened?"

"Yeah. The stage door."

"And the opened door hit your hand so hard it broke it?"

"Well . . . I was kind of reaching for the door, so I guess the combination of my reach, and uh, you know how heavy those stage doors are so, I'm guessing, speculating really, that someone on the other side of the door, not seeing that I was on . . . the other side . . . of the door reaching out my hand, must have pushed pretty hard, so I guess the speed of the door . . . "

The doctor, having none of it, continued:

"Let's check your blood pressure."

He rolled up my shirt sleeve revealing an upper arm of purple, yellow, black, brown, and red with a hint of green, the result of several days of playing the trade-punches-with-Will game.

"What happened here?" the doctor inquired.

I looked at the mass of bruise and confidently announced:

"I have no idea."

I was, I realized, a battered wife.

We shut down production for the day and I was shipped off to Cedars-Sinai Medical Center, where a hand surgeon was standing by.

Will had been the cause of *two* patients being at Cedars that day—me and my broken hand and Jada, giving birth to their son, Jaden.

Will Smith Thinks He Needs to Save My Life

Will and I were coming out of a meeting on the SONY lot. As we were heading to our cars, I asked him to hold up. I had to pee. I picked a tight spot between two diagonally parked cars and started to urinate near the rear tire of a red sports car when a youngish white guy with a goatee headed towards us.

"Hey. What are ya doing?" he yelled in my direction.

I knew from his facial hair he worked in some branch of postproduction.

"Peeing on your car," I honestly yelled back.

I saw Will counting the guy's steps, timing the raising of his fist to meet the car owner's jaw. Will felt it was his responsibility to protect me, annoying as I was. Before an altercation could begin, I zipped my pants, offered an unwashed hand, and said,

"Sorry about that. It's a really nice car. I haven't seen a TR6 that wasn't in a repair shop in decades. I managed to pee only on your tire if that helps. Barry Sonnenfeld. Nice to meet you."

"Barry Sonnenfeld? I love your work. *Get Shorty* is one of my favorite films." He offered me his business card and shook my less than hygienic hand.

"I'm an editor if you're ever looking for one. I'd love to work with you. Don't worry about the car, man."

"Thanks," I said. "This is Will Smith. He thought he was going to have to punch you out because I peed on your tire."

"It would have been an honor," the editor said.

As Will and I continued down the lane of diagonally parked cars, not for the first time, I heard Will mutter:

"White folk."

Sparkle Creek

During the many years I lived in the Hamptons, one of my biggest fears was that Indian Point, a nearby nuclear power plant, would have a meltdown. With only a score of miles as the radioactive crow flies between the plant's location and my house, certain death was a constant worry. The fact that Route 27, the only escape from the 118-mile-long island, unless you owned a boat, was dotted with little blue signs proclaiming "Emergency Escape Corridor" didn't have the calming effect perhaps intended.

What put me over the edge was when Brookhaven Labs, located partway down that "Emergency Escape Corridor," announced their intention to build a superconducting supercollider.

I emailed the chairman of this endeavor and reminded him that certain scientists speculated there was a chance Brookhaven Labs could create a black hole that would *suck up and destroy all matter in our galaxy.*

His response was unsettling:

Yes, it was possible, but the chance of instantaneously deceasing all life on Earth as well as erasing the universe was at best, *a million to one.*

A million to one chance to end *EVERYTHING*? I'm no gambler, but I didn't like those odds.

I called my buddy, screenwriter/director David Koepp, and gave him a bit of Brookhaven's sketchy background, told Dave the response from its CEO, and suggested there was a screwball comedy in all this.

We met a week later at the King Cole Bar at The St. Regis hotel in Midtown Manhattan. Sipping martinis and in my case smoking a Partagas Serie D No. 4 Robusto [this was a long time ago], David told me he loved the idea, but there was a problem. It was such a good premise, if he was going to write it, he also wanted to direct.

We compromised. I would produce. He would direct. We would start by pitching to Disney, where I had an overall movie deal. If after two years of trying to get it made, we were unsuccessful, I would get to be the director and Dave would produce. We'd trade off every two years.

Koepp's resulting script, *The Superconducting Supercollider of Sparkle Creek Wisconsin*, was funny, surreal, and as brilliantly written as anything by Preston Sturges. A wonderful romantic comedy with fast talking smart alecks. This of course meant Disney would never make it.

At the beginning of the third act, when things have gotten particularly out of hand, with floating cows and boyfriends sent to other dimensions, our male lead decides to add an unstable element to the superconducting supercollider soup. A fellow scientist warns him that adding this additional element could create a black hole, wiping out all matter in the universe—ya hear that, Brookhaven?! "That's an old wives' tale," our guy responds. A black dot appears on screen. It grows bigger and eventually swallows up the entire movie screen leaving the viewer in total darkness. After a painfully long wait—in David's script he had six blank pages each with "continued" written on the bottom—a subtitle appears on the screen:

"Thirteen Billion Years Later"

We cut back to the same moment in time, but in this version of reality, our hero doesn't add the unstable element and the movie continues. Disney paid for David's script but decided not to make the movie. I've tried to get it set up at many other studios and streamers, but Disney has attached so much money to it—David's writing fees and the cost of Sonnenfeld/Josephson's production deal, plus constantly accumulating interest—it is unlikely to ever get produced.

A similar situation happened with two other Disney financed screenplays, both written by Stephen Schiff. Schiff wrote a brilliant screenplay for Don DeLillo's *White Noise*, but we were too close to 9/11 and Disney was spooked by a seemingly metaphorical story about a toxic airborne event. [Decades later, a very different movie was made based on the book.] Schiff's adaptation of an unpublished book about Somen Banerjee, the founder of Chippendales, was tonally challenging for Disney as well. Strange they would pay for three unique screenplays and dump all three, but that's the wacky world of the entertainment "business."

Brookhaven is still trying to end it all. In February 2023 it announced its particle accelerator created a substance that hasn't existed for 13 billion years. The substance is believed to be the smallest, hottest, and densest state of our universe—quark-gluon soup.

Good luck to us all.

On Not Directing *Ali*

After *Men in Black*, SONY wanted to find another movie for me. While directing *Wild Wild West*, I read *Ali*, a very good script by Christopher Wilkinson and Stephen Rivele. SONY optioned the script, willing to wait until I finished my western. The first thing Sweetie and I did was to meet Ali at his Hancock Park home. He could not have been more gracious, funny, enthusiastic, sarcastic, and sly. At the meeting was Howard Bingham, the champ's friend and unofficial photographer for decades.

There was a beatific aura emanating from Ali, and just shaking his hand filled you with a peaceful feeling.

Sweetie and I then went through an arduous process trying to convince Will Smith to star in our movie.

He turned us down.

"I can't do better than the real thing," he told us. There had been an extraordinary documentary about the Ali/Foreman fight, *When We Were Kings*, that pretty much told us everything we needed to know about the champ. Still, a feature film starring Will Smith could find a much larger audience.

One night on the set of *Wild Wild West*, waiting for Michael Balhaus to take his multiple hours to light the interior of our train, Sweetie and I stood on stage with Will trying one last time to convince him to play Ali.

Sweetie was particularly articulate.

"Ali is Jesus. His government, religion, even his body turn against him and through it all, the man radiates peace and kindness. There's an important story to be told and someone will play this part. Don't you want it to be you?"

She had been holding Will's upper arm while speaking to him and later confessed she had tried to remove her hand, but a magnetic force literally prevented her from letting go. Will told us he'd sign on. Thank you, Sweetie!

Although John Calley was still the chairman of SONY, he was an excellent delegator and left the daily operation of the film group to Amy Pascal.

Chairperson Amy Pascal and Josh Brolin. Hotel Georges V. Paris. MIB3 junket.

Amy might resent this characterization, but we have certain personality traits in common. We both take our work seriously, but less so ourselves. That is, until someone doesn't take us seriously—then watch out. Amy is a bit of a goofball, as am I. On any given day, you could be meeting with a Chanel-dressed, well-coiffed female executive in charge of a multibillion-dollar company or be sitting opposite a chick whose hair was a fright, decked out in torn jeans, an unbuttoned buffalo plaid shirt jac and a white T-shirt revealing bare midriff.

The morning Will agreed to play Ali, I drove to SONY to tell Amy he would be calling and negotiations could begin. Amy was thrilled by the news and was literally jumping on her couch screaming:

"Best picture, best actor, best director! We're all going to win Academy Awards!"

"Hey Amy," I said. "Let's just make a good movie and not worry about awards, if that's OK with you."

"Sure, Barry. You worry about the picture. I'll worry about the awards."

Wild Wild West was a disappointment. It wasn't a good movie. Although it grossed a quarter of a billion dollars, that was just OK money for 1999. It was an expensive critical and box office failure. It won five Razzies. It was not the movie any of us intended to make.

After its poor reception, I was back home in Amagansett getting ready to start prep on *Ali* when Will called.

"Baz," he said. "We're not doing *Ali* together."

I knew where this was heading, but I played dumb, which wasn't much of a challenge. I wasn't going to make it easy for him.

"Well, Will. I'm sorry to hear that. You would have been fantastic in the role, but I'll look for another actor. I'll miss you, my friend."

"That's not what I'm sayin', Baz."

"Oh?"

"I'm still doing *Ali*. You're not."

Amy Pascal knew the smart money was on Will, not me. I don't blame her for betting on that horse. I was removed from the film and received a fee for the work I had done—convincing the biggest box office star, and the best actor for the role, to play Ali.

Despite how much Will loved *Men in Black*, a movie I had worked hard to cast him in, he disliked *Wild Wild West* equally. In Hollywood, you're only as good as your last movie.

I will never know this as fact, but I believe Will's first choice, after I was fired, was Spike Lee, who had recently worked with his wife, Jada. At the time, Spike was known as an indie director, so if indeed Will had asked for Spike, Amy wasn't interested. Michael Mann was brought on to direct.

Will did a fantastic job as Ali. He was charming and funny, and the boxing matches were acted, choreographed, and directed to perfection. I doubt I could have directed those fights as well as Michael Mann.

The Hits Keep Comin'

Will and I were finishing *Wild Wild West,* and already thinking about *Ali,* the movie I had not yet been fired from. Sadly for me, he brought a couple of inflatable boxing gloves to the *Wild Wild West* ADR stage.

The concept is to fill these huge gloves with air, Velcro them around your wrist, allowing your fist to float inside these comic book balloon-ish orbs, and softly punch your opponent, which would do no harm and definitely not knock them unconscious.

Will has too much energy and only one speed—STUPID.

Instead of having a fun time, softly hitting his opponent with what were in effect balloons, Will hit me so hard the inflatable boxing glove exploded, at which point there was no airbag between the force of his fist and my face.

I awoke face up on the carpeted ADR stage as a grinning Will Smith head came into focus.

"You OK, Baz?" Will laughed.

The Superpowerless Superhero

Barry Josephson and I had two studio deals—Disney for feature films and SONY for television. The TV executive at Sonnenfeld/Josephson was a guy named Flody Suarez, who found us *The Tick*, created by Ben Edlund. I was a big fan of Ben's animated show on Cartoon Network and liked the idea of a live action version. We pitched the show to various networks and the day we met with Fox was the day Sandy Grushow was named its new president. Sandy felt buying our project on his first day in office was a newsworthy move, even though he didn't really understand what he was buying. Once he grasped its concept, he hated it.

After we shot the pilot, it took Sandy a year to order eight additional episodes and put *The Tick* on air.

Sandy hated Ben, me, and the concept of the show. He bought it for the wrong reason and only put it on, briefly, because everyone on his "creative team" loved it.

The surreal highlight of our short life at Fox happened months after we completed the pilot during a heated meeting to discuss future episodes.

Ben and I were in Sandy's office to chat about the Tick's superhero powers:

"He has no superpower," Ben quietly explained.

"What do you mean he has no superpower? He's a fucking superhero! Superheroes have superpowers!"

"Not *all* superheroes have superpowers," said Ben.

"What the hell are you talking about? There's no such thing as a superhero without a superpower."

"Batman," Edlund patiently explained.

"Batman has superpowers!"

"He actually doesn't."

"Of course he does."

"Actually, he doesn't," Ben said once again in a calm, quiet voice.

"This is insane. Are you saying the Tick has no superpowers?"

"He's very strong, if that helps," said Ben.

"In any case, Sandy," I interjected. "It's kind of a semantics issue, isn't it?"

"Fucking idiots," said Sandy, allowing his inner voice to be set free.

Despite Sandy hating the show, I've been told he intended to pick it up for a second season, but SONY, in its wisdom, had decided to get out of the television business.

We had a great cast, led by the brilliant Patrick Warburton playing the Tick. Bo Welch once again was the production designer and suggested costume designer Colleen Atwood, who he had worked with in the past. She designed a blue, one-piece foam latex suit for Warburton that took so long to get on and off Patrick ended up peeing in his suit to save us shooting time.

Liz Vassey was an easy hire for Captain Liberty. She's sassy and talked fast at her audition. It was harder to convince Nestor Carbonell to play Batmanuel. Nestor had a great audition, and we made an offer. His agent called saying Nestor would love to do the part but didn't want to be typecast as Hispanic. Josephson told his agent we'd change his ethnicity, which I thought was nuts. I called Nestor and explained as much as I'd love to work with him, the character's name, for Christ's sake, was Batmanuel and that meant he was Hispanic. Nestor thought about it for ten seconds and came on board. He was great. Finally, we hired David Burke as Arthur, the Tick's sidekick.

The Tick has antennas, and Patrick's were manipulated by radio control, operated by Mark Setrakian, the off-camera puppeteer. Warburton is a perfect comedy actor because he never hits the comedy. He was so in tune with that philosophy that he worried his antennas were being too funny. Although he couldn't see what they were doing, he could hear the servo motors moving his antennas and was concerned they were overacting. I can imagine his discomfort not being in total control of his performance. I also suspect he might have been slightly jealous of his appendages. I promised I wouldn't let his antennas overact, and he trusted me.

I was relatively new to television, having produced and directed *Maximum Bob*, for ABC, and executive produced a remake of *Fantasy Island*, which might still be on the air if we had gone with CBS instead of ABC.

I screwed up on those two adventures and should have stayed more involved in *The Tick*, but I lived on the East Coast, the show shot in LA, and I was lazy and naive. The show's comic tone changed dramatically once we brought on, at Sandy's insistence, Larry Charles to help Ben Edlund run the writer's room. Larry had done great work on *Seinfeld*, but was not the guy for *The Tick*. Larry brought real, modern aspects to the show instead of letting the Tick exist in his own quirky world, and it kinda got ruined.

Bad Timing for a Good Movie

I directed one movie during my three-year deal at Disney. *Big Trouble* was based on a novel by Dave Barry with a funny plot full of wacky Floridians. Ronna Kress and I put together a great cast:

Tim Allen, Rene Russo, Stanley Tucci, Sofia Vergara, Tom Sizemore, Johnny Knoxville, Dennis Farina, Janeane Garofalo, Patrick Warburton, Ben Foster, Zooey Deschanel, DJ Qualls, Heavy D, Omar Epps, Jason Lee, Andy Richter, and an uncredited Martha Stewart.

I had wanted Alec Baldwin for the lead but Disney insisted on Tim Allen.

The plot revolved around a mysteriously heavy metal suitcase that unbeknownst to our characters, contained a nuclear bomb.

Tom Sizemore had a reputation for being "difficult," but he wanted a part. We met in my Disney office, and I agreed to hire him under two conditions:

1. He had to do whatever I told him, and
2. He had to promise he would never hit me.

After our first day of filming in Miami, I called him to my trailer: "Hey Tom. I have to fire you."

"Why?" he bellowed, his face turning red while his eyes bugged out like a cartoon character.

"You're trying to be funny."

"It's a comedy!" he screamed.

"And that's why you decided your character has a limp and a twitch?"

"Yeah. It's funny!"

"Don't be funny. Just play the scene. Be real. The more you try to be funny, it's . . . it's . . . *HORRIBLE*."

"But, Knoxville is funny."

"Right. He's funny because he's not trying to be funny. He's just playing the scene based on his character."

"I don't know what the fuck you're talking about," Tom said, literally foaming at the corners of his mouth.

"Look. I'll give you one more day. You're a good actor, Tom. Just don't be funny. OK?"

"OK," Tom yelped, as he slammed the camper's door on the way out.

Tom took my direction and was actually good in the movie.

Tim Allen and Robin Williams, who I would direct down the road on *RV*, had similar personalities. One on one, both were smart, quiet, interesting guys. Tim's interests were watches, pens, and cars. Robin went with watches, pens, and bicycles. Both had a biological imperative to perform as soon as there was more than one person present.

Tim was a handful on set. He was loud and his jokes were repetitive and sometimes mean. In addition, he liked to ad-lib while doing his off-camera lines, which makes no sense and just confuses the on-camera actor.

I stopped bringing Tim to the set to read his off-camera lines and had the script supervisor read in his stead.

We were filming the scene where Rene and Tim meet for the first time. It's important that we sense instant chemistry between the two. The three Barrys—Josephson, Barry Fanaro [the uncredited writer], and I watched Rene and Tim rehearse.

"OK. Great. Hey Tim, you need to be instantly smitten with Rene."

"Why would I be?" asked Tim.

"Well, she's beautiful and in the previous scene where you first saw her she was funny and witty . . ."

"I'm not attracted to her," he said about one of the most beautiful women I've worked with—in front of that very beautiful woman.

"I'll act attractive, Tim. I promise," Rene whispered in a sultry Marilyn Monroe voice.

"It's hard to act attracted to someone if they're not attractive."

"You're an actor, Tim. Just act like you're attracted to one of the most beautiful women in the world. OK?!"

"I can try," Tim said helpfully.

I apologized to Rene, who seemed more amused than hurt by this mean human, and we got through the shoot.

Publicity shoot: Knoxville, Sizemore, Foster, Allen, Russo, Deschanel, D, Epps.

Most actors and crew hate filming at night, but I love it. Much of the crew became a tad psychotic, since our schedule called for 58 nights out of a 60 day schedule. I don't sleep much in any case, so nights were fine with me. Nighttime Miami has a wonderful loamy smell and a humidity that is almost visible. The other advantage of filming at night is the temperature's 20 degrees cooler than during the day.

The only disadvantage of night shooting is at the end of 12 hours of filming, I like to have a cocktail, but drinking a martini as the sun comes up just didn't feel right.

The film was funny and quirky. Dave Barry and Barry Fanaro wrote great dialogue and we had a bevy of wonderful actors. The challenge was that quirky movies are hard to market and definitely not Disney's métier.

But that was the least of our problems. What sunk our movie was 9/11. Our original release date was September 21, 2001, and we couldn't release a film about a suitcase nuclear bomb *on an airplane* ten days after the demise of the twin towers. When the movie *was* released in April 2002, with virtually no money spent on advertising, one of the entertainment shows—perhaps *Extra?*—intercut our trailer with footage of the falling towers, with their host asking if America was ready for a comedy about 9/11.

Disney spent so little money marketing the movie it just printed a patch with a new date, gluing it onto the former movie banners that previously hung in theaters.

Big Trouble is one of my favorite movies.

The Villain Should Sell Ice Cream

One night I entered a sushi restaurant in Beverly Hills and saw Walter Parkes, Laurie MacDonald, and Sherry Lansing, along with her husband, William Friedkin, at a power table.

I walked over to my three nemeses and with open arms and a cheerful demeanor proclaimed:

"One table. Three of my favorite people!"

The group appreciated my irony.

After not talking for several years, Walter and I had lunch two weeks later at The Buffalo Club in Santa Monica.

He admitted my work on the first *Men in Black* was excellent but was angry I didn't give him enough credit in interviews. I promised I would do better if there ever was a next one. I will end up reneging on that promise.

I liked Walter. I just didn't enjoy working with him. But as a guy to eat a meal or take a road trip with, I'm in.

Somehow Walter convinced Amy Pascal, SONY's chairperson, to develop the sequel with *no* input from me. After years of development, I received a copy of the *Men in Black II* script from Walter. Amy proclaimed she loved it and wanted *MIB II* released on the July 4th weekend, in less than a year and a half. To make that date, we needed to start preproduction immediately. SONY made deals with Will, Tommy, and me.

The *MIB II* script Walter had developed needed A LOT of work. I think there were zombies in it.

"Amy. I can't direct this script. It is full of gags and doesn't reflect our tone or characters."

"Hire any writer you want," said Amy, "but we need to begin prepping this show right away so you can't start from scratch."

"Ames. The script is bad. It's a big mistake to back into a release date. Let's get the script better first."

"You'll figure it out," which was a very Amy response. "We need to release it a year from this July."

I asked Barry Fanaro to help. Barry and I met Walter and Laurie at their house in Santa Monica to make sure they felt comfortable with Fanaro and the script changes we had in mind.

We sat in the living room.

"Grammy has a great idea," Walter proudly announced.

"Great. What is it?"

"I'm going to let Grammy tell you himself."

In walked their 10ish-year-old son, Graham.

"The villain should sell ice cream. From one of those ice cream trucks."

"And . . . ?" I asked.

"The truck could have a creepy jingle that always plays when it arrives somewhere."

"Pretty great?" uh-huhed Walter.

Barry and I weren't completely stupid so we offered an "It *was* pretty great!" and "We'll see what we could do with it."

Grammy had to skip the rest of the meeting for a play date, so any further script discussion was tabled on account of no Grammy.

Amy remained in a hurry to get started and arranged for the SONY jet to fly Barry and me back to my place in East Hampton where we were supposed to make the script substantially better without changing much. The script got better, but not nearly good enough. We really needed to throw out the draft and come up with a different idea but Amy refused that kind of major surgery. The evil ice cream man didn't make it into the next draft. With a script none of us loved, we set off to start *Men in Black II*.

Will and I had not yet resolved our disagreeable ending to *Ali*.

We were civil but weren't having fun. It felt like a business relationship, which was quite different from the close, funny friendship we had on the first one.

Will was floundering. There was neither energy nor joy in his performance.

Two weeks into the show we were shooting a night scene at the Empire Diner on Tenth Avenue and 22nd Street in New York. It was a good scene between Will and his partner, played by Patrick Warburton. The scene ends with Will neuralyzing Warburton, telling him to fall in love with the waitress, played by Sasha Erwitt, my stepdaughter.

We broke for lunch around 1 AM. As Sweetie and I raced across Tenth Avenue to get out of a sudden summer downpour, Will ran out of the diner and grabbed us. We stood in the curb lane, the three of us getting soaked, as Will, his wet face a combination of rain and tears, apologized about *Ali*.

"I was weak," he sobbed. "I was wrong. Please forgive me," he begged.

"It's OK, Will. It's fine."

"OK, Baz. I just want things to be better with us."

We all hugged.

Will thanked Sweetie and me for understanding and raced to his trailer.

"Should we move on?" I asked Sweetie.

We stood in the rain, once again feeling the pain that Will's firing had caused us, once again deciding to take it on the chin.

We moved on.

Michael Jackson Twelve Years Later

Amy Pascal called. Michael Jackson, whose record deal was at SONY MUSIC, wanted to be in *Men in Black II*, and both SONY MUSIC and Pascal really wanted this to happen. I offered Michael a role as an alien [no brainer] but he insisted on being an MIB agent, which was tougher for me to swallow. Directing the first *Men in Black*, I had tried to convince Michael to be an alien on the big board when Will Smith is shown famous people who are really aliens: George Lucas, Spielberg, Al Roker, DeVito, my baby Chloe, Stallone, Isaac Mizrahi . . . Michael didn't feel being an alien was on brand.

Really?

Now, five years later, he wanted to wear the black suit. Amy thought his appearance in a hit movie would be great [for him]; I wondered if he was slightly damaged goods.

Since Pascal rarely met a star she didn't want to please, Michael got to join the Men in Black.

"Amy Pascal, please," I spoke into my cell phone.

"What?!" Amy impatiently asked.

"Number One won't come out of his trailer."

"Will won't come out of his trailer?"

"Not Will. Michael Jackson! We're required to call him Number One. Number One. The King of Pop. Did you not get the memo?"

"That's ridiculous."

"*Ya think?*! Hey Amy. Any chance you could, you know, as chairman, and as the single reason we agreed to this insanity, come down and have a chat with him? We've been waiting over an hour."

"Your job. You do it. I'll come down when you're done. I want to thank him . . . and give him his suit."

Michael finally arrived on set. In red pajamas.

I instructed him to place his feet on a piece of tape that marked where to stand. He would be in a medium close-up. Although we were on the main Men in Black Headquarters set, we placed Michael in front of blue screen. My plan was to have him reporting from Antarctica, surrounded by penguins. He would be talking to an off-camera Zed, played by the almost certifiably insane Rip Torn.

The King of Pop, standing on his mark, stared out at dozens of crew members and whispered:

"Mr. Barry. Can we do this tomorrow?"

"Let's take a walk Number One. The cinematographer needs a minute to adjust the lights and you need to get into wardrobe."

Back in Michael's camper, the King of Pop started to weep.

"But, Mr. Barry. Can it be tomorrow?"

"I'm sorry, Michael, um, King. It has to be today. But if you don't want to do it, we can make it work without you."

"Mr. Barry. This is my dream. From the time I was a little boy— to be an agent of Men in Black."

"Well, the first movie just came out five years ago so you weren't a little . . . , but yeah, I get what you mean."

"Please," Number One begged.

"We kind of have to do this now or move on. I'm sorry, Michael."

"OK, Mr. Barry. I understand."

I left Michael's trailer and walked back to the set. The first assistant director told me to call Pascal immediately.

"Did you just fire Michael?"

"Do you mean Number One? King of Pop?"

"He just told me you said you would do it without him. What the fuck are you doing down there?!"

"Well, *he* said he wanted to do it tomorrow, which obviously doesn't work. So I told him he had to do it today or not at all. But I did not, believe me, fire him."

"Fix this!" Amy impatiently yelled.

I went back to the King of Pop's trailer and somehow convinced him to put on the fucking black suit and walked him to the set.

Number One on set.

We rolled camera.

"Zeke?"

"Cut."

"Hey Mich . . . Number One. His name is Zed. Zed. Roll camera . . . and . . . ACTION."

"Zeke?"

"Cut. Sorry. It's Zed. Call him Zed."

"Zeke?"

"Why the fuck does he keep calling me Zeke?" Rip roared.

I could tell Michael was nervous. He was a frightened delicate child.

"Hey, so, sorry to keep cutting, but you need to call him Zed. That's the character's name. Zed."

"Mr. Barry. Can't you change his name? It seems Zeke is a much better name."

"Yeah, well, unfortunately, Number One, we've already established, in two movies, that his name is Zed."

"Doesn't Zeke work just as well?"

"Sorry, King. You've got to call him Zed."

This one shot took several more hours.

It was worth it when I received the following handwritten note on bright red paper from M. Jackson:

Barry.
I Love you.
You Made My Dream Come True.
Love
M. Jackson

Tommy Waxes Philosophically

Will bounded out of his camper at 2:30 AM to pitch me the plot of *Men in Black 3*, which we would film a decade later. The night was soft and warm, which was unusual for LA. Greg Gardiner, the cinematographer, was lighting the set. We knew Greg was close to being ready since he usually was engaged in a nonstop dialogue with himself:

"I could put a double net in the 10K but maybe I could achieve the same thing by pulling a double from the 5K but if I did that, would I have enough exposure to carry the depth of field between Tommy and Will? Actually, I'd have more exposure, not less, wouldn't I?"

The first assistant director overheard Greg convincing Greg he was close to ready and called for Tommy Lee Jones to come to set. Tommy showed up and sat between Will and me.

"Hey, Tommy. Tell me why life is like a tampon."

I truly have no idea why I asked this stupid question and did not expect an answer.

Without hesitation Tommy offered:

"You know, Barry. Life is like a tampon. You're always in the best possible place at the worst possible time."

Will fell out of his chair.

The Little Shit

We were once again at Todd-AO, this time re-recording dialogue for *Men in Black II*. In attendance was Will Smith, his wife, Jada, and his formidable assistant, Charlie Mack.

The Smiths wanted takeout food from Mr. Chow, an expensive Chinese restaurant in Beverly Hills. I gave Will a couple of things I liked [green shrimp, gambler's duck], then let him order the rest, which meant he chose extremely high-priced food for everyone working on the show that day—the two picture editors, the dialogue editor, our ADR editor, various technicians from Todd-AO, and of course, Charlie. All I know about Will's order is that the total came to $1,300. Will handed me the bill. I paid with my credit card and submitted the $1,300 invoice for reimbursement, which was paid by the *MIB II* accountant.

A couple of weeks later, Gary Martin, president of physical production at SONY, called.

"Is this the Little Shit?" Gary asked.

"Hi, Gar. Yes it is!"

"I'm looking over your fucking movie's cost report and I see you and your friend managed to spend thirteen hundred bucks for Chinese food and expect me to pay for it."

"Well not you, Gar. The studio."

"You've got an hour to get a check for thirteen hundred fucking dollars made out to SONY Pictures over to my office. Got it?"

"You bet, Gar. I mean, I suspect it won't help if I told you that it was Will who . . . "

"An hour."

For several years my assistant was a very handsome and charming Quebecois, David Alexandre. Charming is not a word usually associated with French speaking Quebecois, and I should know, having had one of the worst experiences of my career filming *Nine Lives* in Montreal. One of David's jobs was carrying around my martini kit. It was always thrilling to have a meeting with a studio executive and offer up a martini. As if they were being very naughty, they'd whisper, "Do you think we should?"

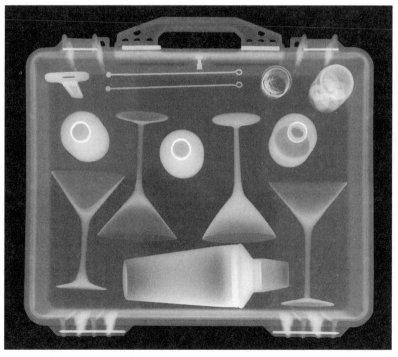

X-ray of my martini kit.

The Pelican case held a shaker, four martini glasses, olives, toothpicks, and three small bottles of vodka all enrobed in foam.

David would call the exec's assistant beforehand to make sure there was ice. His presentation, with a bar towel draped over his forearm, a brutally shaken martini in each hand, was perfection.

On this day, instead of carrying martinis, David was hand delivering my personal check for $1,300 to Gary Martin.

"How did it go?" I asked David, upon his return to my office.

David handed me a ripped-up check.

"Gary said, and these are his words, not mine . . .'I just wanted to see if the Little Shit was man enough to write me a check.'"

He was.

On Not Directing Jim Carrey, Part 1

I blame the flu for agreeing to direct *Fun with Dick and Jane*.

At some point in late 2002 I was in East Hampton lying in bed, sick and feverish, when Amy Pascal called and asked me to direct *Fun with Dick and Jane*. There was one big issue: It was starring Jim Carrey and he had an outdate, meaning we'd have to finish filming the movie by a certain date. I would have to start shooting in ten weeks. I told Amy two and a half months was not enough prep time considering how much work the script needed. Also, like *Men in Black II*, we were shoehorning ourselves into a start date that had nothing to do with a good script. Hadn't we learned that a good script is more important than a specific release date?

Amy can be very persuasive, and I agreed to start preproduction with the mutual understanding that the script required a big rewrite.

The show was being produced by Imagine Films, owned by Ron Howard and Brian Grazer. I had worked with them on my second directorial effort, *For Love or Money*. Brian must have forgotten what I'd said about him in *Premiere* magazine:

"Brian Grazer is an idiot savant, without the savant part."

Soon after the story ran, Brian sent me a fax [this was pre-email]:

Dear Barry. Fuck you. Fuck you. Fuck you.

I called Brian: "Brian. It was a joke. If I really felt that way, do you think I'd actually say it?"

Brian decided I didn't really think he was an idiot [he's not] and we moved on.

Michael Tolkin, the excellent screenwriter, and I met to discuss a rewrite of the screenplay. He had great ideas and Amy loved him. A meeting was set at Jim Carrey's rental house in the famous Malibu Colony.

The Malibu Colony is a small, gated community of funky houses on the Pacific Ocean. *The Long Goodbye*, directed by Robert Altman, starring Elliott Gould and former Yankee pitcher Jim Bouton, had many scenes that took place at the Colony.

Several things went wrong that afternoon: My assistant gave Tolkin the wrong address—it was a lane/boulevard/street/terrace kind of mistake; there was no cell service at the Colony so Michael couldn't find us, and when he eventually did arrive, he was sweating, wearing a tweed jacket with elbow patches.

Jim felt an instant "not hip," professor vibe and didn't want to work with him. So there went that.

We hired two writers associated with Jim: Judd Apatow and Nick Stoller. Judd would supervise, Nick would write. I met with them, gave my notes, and stressed that the comedy needed to be reality-based. No gags. No silly stuff. No jokes.

I then had a second meeting back in Malibu with Carrey, his manager [no longer his, now mine] Jimmy Miller, Grazer, SONY executive Doug Belgrad, and Amy. I laid it out for everybody:

"Here's the problem. Jim thinks he's hiring Barry Sonnenfeld to direct a Jim Carrey movie, and I think Jim has been hired to act in a Barry Sonnenfeld movie. Those are two very different movies. I need to know that Jim understands the script needs to reflect my taste, not his."

Jim got down on his knees as if Al Jolson and sang a song about how I'm in charge, and he understands my insecurities, and he'll get me coffee, and call me "sir" [crew code for asshole].

Pure Jim Carrey schtick.

He finished to a big round of applause. [Not from me.]

I asked Grazer to take a walk.

"So what's your thinking, Brian? Are you looking for a goofy Jim Carrey movie, or a reality-based but funny Barry Sonnenfeld movie? What's your opinion?"

Brian can be disarmingly honest:

"I don't have an opinion until I see who wins. Once I know if it's Jim or you, then that's my opinion. At the moment, you're both right."

I left the Colony after reminding Pascal that there wasn't a lot of time for script revisions, and if the next draft didn't reflect the tone I requested, I wasn't going to direct the film.

Amy said she understood. If the next draft didn't achieve what I asked for, she acknowledged I would leave the show. At least that's what she said.

I continued to cast and location scout, which was hard since there were so many unknowns. We needed a house, and I knew we would build the interiors, so I focused on that. We auditioned actors whose characters seemed likely to remain in the film. A couple of weeks later the new draft came in and it definitely reflected Jim's vision of the movie, not mine—it had rocket powered roller blades.

I called Amy and told her there was no time left; the new draft, although funny, wasn't the kind of funny I knew how to direct and that as we had agreed, since the script didn't get closer to my requests, I was quitting. Amy was furious.

I had convinced Cameron Diaz to co-star in the film. She wasn't into it, but felt Jim made her career with *The Mask* and she owed him. Once Cameron heard I had left, that was her out. SONY started from scratch and hired a lovely guy, Dean Parisot, to direct. Tea Leoni, a very talented actress, took over for Ms. Diaz.

More than a year and a half later, I was in Alberta, Canada, in late winter, scouting locations for *RV*, which was going to start filming that summer with Robin Williams. We met a location scout who had the keys to open the gate to Lake Kananaskis [insert a Robin Williams' joke about the lake's name here, usually a version of, "Can an ass kiss? If it puckers up, it can."].

The scout told me he had a message from Dean Parisot, whom he had worked with on *Fun with Dick and Jane.* Thanks to Jim the picture was rumored to have been a nightmare, going tens of millions of dollars over budget—two of Jim's requirements were that all sets had to be warmed or cooled to exactly 63 degrees and a helicopter had to be on standby to fly fresh fruit and vegetables from the Imperial Valley to the set within an hour of picking.

"I know the message."

"I don't think you do. Dean gave it to me last night, on the phone."

"Is it three words?"

"Actually, it is."

"'You were right.'"

"Wow. That's the message."

On Not Directing Jim Carrey, Part 2

The second me-almost-directing-a-Jim-Carrey-film was Paramount's *A Series of Unfortunate Events*. I had read the books to my daughter, Chloe, years earlier and loved them. The novels posit that adults, whether they mean well or not, are fundamentally ineffectual [my parents] while children are capable and resourceful [my kids].

Scott Rudin had produced the two *Addams Family* movies at Paramount and I was happy to work with him again. I thought John Turturro would be an excellent Count Olaf, but Sherry Lansing and Scott insisted on a name. They wanted Jim Carrey. The studio also wanted to make the movie at a low budget.

Jim Carrey's participation and "low budget" are oxymoronic.

Sherry was quite capable of embracing these two totally contradictory thoughts and felt it was my job to make both work. It is the actual definition of both insanity and Hollywood.

As the budget for the movie climbed, Scott bailed. I was now in preproduction on a film with no producer. I suspect Scott was fed up working on the script with Daniel Handler, author of the books and now the screenplay. It was hard to get Daniel to understand a book and movie are not the same thing, and Daniel was very protective of his books. Getting him to rewrite his script was tedious and contentious.

I was fluent in Sherry. Her MO was the same as my mother's and Scott's. All three had a fluid relationship with the truth. If a lie achieved your goal, it was the truth.

After Rudin departed, Sherry called:

"Barry. I have never made a black comedy that made money."

"Yes, you have. I directed two of them."

"Never."

"*Addams Family* and *Addams Family Values.*"

"Oh, honey. They don't count."

"Why not?"

"In any case, [Sherry is about to take a neck-wrenching hard left turn to avoid that line of questioning], we need a partner. I can't make this movie unless another studio comes in and co-finances with us."

"OK. Give me a week."

I sent the script to SONY. They were in. Their only stipulation: SONY's bylaws let them co-finance up to $50 million of their money, which meant if the movie ballooned to over $100 million, they couldn't put in any additional cash. However, if we went over $100 million, SONY was willing to dilute their 50 percent profit participation proportionately. Sherry declined the offer.

"OK, Sherry. If you want to try another studio, go ahead, just don't go to DreamWorks, because if you do, Walter Parkes [who was running the studio] will fire me the next day."

I was in Las Vegas when Sweetie answered the phone in our suite. I was there covering the Consumer Electronics Show for *Esquire* magazine, something I'd been doing every year for the past decade.

"It's Melanie," Sweetie said, holding out the phone.

Melanie Cook was my entertainment lawyer for 20 years, and I knew this wasn't good news. My sciatica was already in full swing from walking the floor of the Las Vegas Convention Center, stressed at having to write a review comparing the Pioneer Elite, Sharp Aquos, and SONY Bravia 55 inch LCD televisions. The Pioneer Elite, by the way, was the best of the bunch.

I knew what this call meant.

"Hey Mel."

"Hey Bear."

"Should I guess?"

"No. I'll tell you. I just got off the phone with Sherry. Paramount is going to partner with DreamWorks."

"I saw that coming."

"Sherry says you quit."

"Riiiiiight," I replied.

"So I said, 'Barry didn't quit. You're firing him.'"

Sherry said, "Quit. Fired. What difference does it make?"

"It makes a big difference. Financially," I told Sherry.

"She said, 'Fine. Sue us. In any case, he's off the picture.'"

Years later Walter and I temporarily declared a truce so we could find a way to do *Men in Black 3* together. I asked Walter if he really thought Brad Silberling, the eventual director of *A Series of Unfortunate Events*, was a better director than me.

"Of course not! I was punishing you," he admitted.

Consumer Electronics Show. Las Vegas.

The Kosher Cowboy

It had been more than three years since the release of *Men in Black II*. The triple header of *Wild Wild West* followed by Disney's dumping of *Big Trouble* and a mediocre *Men in Black* sequel cooled any heat I had.

Lucy Fisher, my advocate at SONY when she ran the studio under Mark Canton, along with her husband, the dry witted Doug Wick, were now producers at the studio. They asked me to fly to LA and meet Robin Williams, hoping he'd approve me to direct *RV*. Robin and I hit it off and I was hired.

Due to the strong US vs Canadian dollar, plus certain British Columbia tax credits, SONY wanted us to film this very American road movie exclusively in Canada.

I begged Gary Martin, SONY's head of physical production, to give us the 54 million dollar budget and let me decide where to film. Maybe we could save even more money in the States. Gary, under pressure from the studio to reduce its budgets, liked the optics of the BC tax incentives. He was also fond of the favorable US vs Canadian dollar exchange rates and put his foot down; we were filming in Canada.

Me on my DIRECTOR's golf cart. [Also me on the side of the RV in the background.]

That summer, British Columbia set a record of 57 straight days of rain. *In the summer dry season!* The show was difficult not only because of weather but also due to Robin's anger and unhappiness. Years after our movie was released, a now sober Robin Williams called to apologize for swearing at me in front of children and for being such a total dick on the show. His personal issues and drug use made working with him difficult, but he was fine in the movie. The rest of the cast were so much fun that I looked forward to any day Robin wasn't on set.

For a while, Thomas Haden Church was going to play Travis Gornicke, husband to Kristin Chenoweth's Mary Jo. We were close to a deal when Mr. Church called. He realized, he pontificated, after *Sideways* he had to be careful about his next career move and feared his fans didn't want to see him in *RV*. They had higher aspirations.

Ronna Kress, our casting director, suggested Jeff Daniels. Knowing I had a singing dynamo in Chenoweth, I was curious what Jeff could add musically.

"So, Jeff. I listened to your records, and you're a fantastic singer/songwriter. It might be fun if you, Kristin, and your three movie kids sang a song at the campground."

"Sounds great," Jeff offered.

"Any chance you play the banjo?"

"In fact, I do."

"Any chance you can also, at the same time, play one of those harmonicas around your neck like Bob Dylan?"

"I see where this is going," said Jeff. "Sure I can."

Jeff, Chenoweth, and the three Gornicke kids, one of whom was my daughter Chloe, sang a beautiful rendition of Delaney & Bonnie's "Never Ending Song of Love." Kristen surprised and delighted with her insane yodeling talent.

While filming exteriors in Lethbridge—the locals called it Deathbridge, claiming it had the highest suicide rate in Alberta because of the incessant prairie winds—Jeff would find a rock to sit on and strum his guitar. Never one to let an actor just chill, I waddled up to him one rare dry afternoon and asked if he could write a short theme song Paul Shaffer could play over my entrance the next time I was on the Letterman show. Instead, Jeff wrote a wonderfully observed full blown song called "The Ballad of the Kosher Cowboy."

There goes the Kosher Cowboy.
He's got his Sweetie by his side.
Though he's sunscreen pale,
He's blazed a trail,
From the Hamptons to Telluride.

For a high plains Hebrew,
His patience is thin,
For no one outmasters the master,
When the pace is draggin',
He circles the wagons,
And says this time, do it faster.

And many more verses.

Jeff might be the easiest actor I've ever directed. After a take where I felt he wasn't at his best, my only direction was:

"Hey Jeff. Be more like Travis [his character's name]."

He'd nod in agreement, and his next take would be perfect.

As part of *RV*'s marketing campaign, I was invited to appear on *The Late Show with David Letterman*. I was played out by Paul Shaffer's rendition of Jeff's "Kosher Cowboy," and I was an absolute horror. It is an extremely painful memory. I was a mean, rotten, whiny baby. I made fun of SONY, showing Dave and the audience photos of various pouring rain locations. I explained in boring detail how stupid it was making me shoot this movie in Canada. I could not have done more to hurt the movie and sully my career. I walked off stage, getting a "nice job" pat on my back from Biff, the show's famous stage manager, and wished I was dead.

A month later, Jeff sent me a framed xeroxed copy of the 99¢ ASCAP royalty check he received for Paul Shaffer's performing "Kosher Cowboy." At least Jeff got something out of my Letterman appearance.

Proof of Concept

For about a decade I would take a biannual drive between my homes in Telluride, Colorado, and East Hampton, Long Island, with Lucky, my 110-pound Rhodesian Ridgeback. At some point along that interstate slog, I got an idea for a television show: interview famous people while taking them on a road trip. The longer, the better: endless hours of driving would be both banal and dynamic. Banal in that given enough mind-numbing hours traversing Interstate 80, my guest would eventually spill their guts:

"You probably want to know about that time I made out with Rihanna," they'd blurt out.

Dynamic because each time we'd stop for gas, we would un-lap all the weird cars and trucks we passed hours earlier, like the chartreuse Peterbilt tractor trailer transporting obese turkeys

. . . or the wide load transporting an alien eyeball, surely on its way to Canada.

In late spring 2006, I shot a proof-of-concept episode. I drove my Honda Ridgeline pickup truck, my dog Lucky, and Neil Kraft, a friend from the Hamptons on my bi-yearly journey to Telluride. We used three cameras: two on the windshield and one handheld. Neil insisted we take the southern route, passing through Memphis so we could stop at Graceland. I don't recommend the detour.

We never should have spent the night in Amarillo.

It was about 5:30 PM when Neil and I checked into a Hampton Inn. Our rooms were in different wings. I dropped off Neil and agreed to meet at 6 PM for dinner in the motel's restaurant. I parked in front of my room, which had direct access to the parking lot.

Next to the Ridgeline was an empty parking space and next to that, an old red pickup with a mass murderer in the driver's seat staring at Lucky and me. The killer's beard was worthy of ZZ Top. His face was cracked leather, probably as tough as his attitude towards New Yorkers. And then there was the gun rack across his rear window. With several rifles.

"Nice dog."

"Oh? Yeah? Thanks."

"Does he like raw meat?"

"Sorry?"

"Would he like some raw meat? I've got access to some."

"Um. He's really not that kind of dog. Mainly dried dog food with the occasional deer poop appetizer."

"Amuse-bouche."

"Huh?"

"The deer poop."

"Right."

"Dog needs raw meat. Especially a big dog. Like that one."

"I'm sure you're right."

"I can give him some raw meat. I bet he'd like it."

"Well, it's a long trip, and um, I'd hate for his stomach to . . . you know . . . eating something he's not used to and then . . . well, you know . . ."

"Suit yeself."

"But really, thanks just the same."

"That your friend? He drivin' with you? The short guy you dropped off on the other side of the inn?"

"Yeah, that's him. Just this *huge antisocial* dog and my friend."

"Where ya'll headin'?"

"Ummm . . . Telluride," I insanely told the man who was going to kill me.

"Beautiful part of the world, I hear. Might need to head up there. Maybe soon."

Lucky pretending to be a guard dog. Texas.

I walked Lucky into the motel room, which meant the bearded gentleman clocked exactly where I was staying. I made a couple of trips back to the truck for camera equipment and laptops, displaying just how much booty he could steal. On my last excursion I noticed Charlie Manson was gone. His truck was still there, but the killer had disappeared.

I called Neil's room to tell him there was a scary overly inquisitive guy who, at a minimum, had dog poison and multiple long guns and intended to kill us. Neil didn't answer the hotel phone, which was unsettling.

I tried his cell.

No answer.

At this point, I knew the following:

1. Neil is dead.
2. The killer intends to poison Lucky with spiked raw meat.

3.   Once Lucky dies a horrible death, the Unabomber intends to kill me and steal my stuff.

Facing my imminent demise I called Sweetie, who was still in the Hamptons preparing to fly to Colorado the next morning. She was having dinner, ironically, with Neil's wife, Scott. Perhaps Scott had heard from Neil. And if not, I guess Sweetie was going to have to give Mrs. Kraft the bad news about her newly deceased husband.

Sweetie didn't answer *her* phone. Where is everybody?!

I left a message:

"Sweetie. I love you so much," I managed to squeak out. "By the time you hear this message, Lucky and I will be dead. Some deranged psychopath . . . Some psychopath . . . In fact, Sweetie, Neil is already dead. He doesn't answer his cell or his room phone, so, um . . . you know. I'm so, so, so sorry, Sweetie. I love you. I love Chloe. Sasha . . . Amy. It's been a great ride. I'm just so, so . . . . sorry."

It was close to 6 PM. I peeked out the window to make sure Ted Bundy was gone.

Heading towards the open-to-the-lobby restaurant I spotted the killer sitting in a semicircular booth. Before I could duck behind a pillar, he saw and waved me over.

Sitting at the booth, his back towards my arrival, was Neil.

"Hey, Ba. This guy wants to give Lucky some raw meat."

"Yeah," said Mr. ZZ Top. "I'm the chef here. Don't start 'til six but like to get to work early, sit in my car and read. I've got two big dogs myself. Both Great Danes. They love it when I bring home meat, and I saw your dog—not as big as mine two, but I thought, I bet he'd like some real food. I met your friend here and since the place is still empty, thought I'd chat. Don't run into many Jews in this part of the world."

"Hey, Neil. Where were you? I called your room. Your cell."

Neil held up an Ethernet cable. "My room didn't have a cable for the internet so I got one from the front desk [this is pre-hotel Wi-Fi]. I left my cell phone in the room, and it was close enough to six I figured I'd just start drinking without you. So, what's good here, Jeremy? I'm not a meat eater, raw or cooked."

When I got back to my room, I reached Sweetie and I apologized for what was surely a very unsettling voice mail.

"You know what, Barry? I wasn't worried."

Five and a half years later, on New Year's Day, Jerry Seinfeld, my Telluride neighbor, asked if we could take a drive. He had shipped out his Porsche 911 Twin Turbo with snow tires, and we drove to Rico, a very small town about 40 minutes south. There was something he wanted to run by me. We found a hipster coffee shop that surely wouldn't be in business much longer.

Jerry. Rico, Colorado. January 1, 2012.

"So, I have this idea," Jerry said.

"I know the idea."

"You can't know the idea. I haven't told you yet."

"I know your idea because it's the same one I have."

"You have the same idea as the one I haven't told you?"

"Yup."

"OK, Sonnenfeld. You go first."

"Your idea, same as mine, is to do an interview show while driving in a car. The longer the drive the better. It's both banal and dynamic. That's my idea."

"Mine is completely different," Jerry offered. "Mine is filming me and another comedian driving in a car to get some coffee."

"Ah. Totally different."

Jerry went on to make his show. It was successful and very funny.

Faster. Flatter. Part 1

Surprisingly, casting *Pushing Daisies* was a challenge. Many actors and actresses passed. In fact, we were down to the wire on a male lead. The producers and I had a casting session scheduled for Monday morning with Peter Roth, chairman of Warner Bros. TV, to be followed by a session with Steve McPherson, the feared president of the ABC Television Network. It was Friday, and there was no actor we loved enough to bring to the studio or ABC. Bryan Fuller, the creator and show runner, suggested we make a tentative deal [pending studio approval] with a guy I had never heard of—Lee Pace. Bryan had written and produced a show starring Lee called *Wonderfalls*. At this point, why not.

Lee arrived in Los Angeles Sunday night, just in time to rehearse with Cami, the casting director, producers Bruce Cohen, Dan Jinks, Bryan Fuller, and me. We met at the Graciela, "the only luxury boutique hotel in Burbank," it claimed. Lee knocked on the door to my "suite" around 10 PM, ready to start.

Cami read with Lee. I started to panic halfway through the scene. Lee was painfully slow. Profoundly lethargic. There was a lot of "acting" going on. What seemed like hours later, Lee finished the three-page scene.

"OK. That was great," I lied.

"Here's what I'm thinking: Let's do the scene again but read your lines, like, I don't know, ten thousand times faster."

Lee, in that way an actor can look at a director, narrowed his eyes, very slowly and importantly tilted his head, and asked:

"Just a question: faster because I'm lying to Chuck [eventually played by Anna Friel], or faster because I'm nervous, or because I'm hiding something from her, or perhaps I want to get rid of her?"

"I don't care. Just like a billion times faster."

Lee and Cami read the scene again.

It went ever so slightly faster.

"OK. Great. Cami, perhaps you can pick up your cues, which would mean, Lee, you should pick up your cues as well, and maybe, in addition to losing the dead space between when Cami finishes her lines and when you start yours, you could also just speed up your words, you know, the actual words you're saying, by, oh . . . let's say . . . like a trillion times."

"Got it," said Lee. "Just curious . . . "

God, no.

"Is it because I'm scared of her? Apprehensive? Or am I just not used to talking to people in general?"

"I don't care. Just talk a whole lot faster."

"Great."

I admit my direction of "I don't care. Just talk a whole lot faster" is a bit dickish, but I was tired, and the truth is I wasn't sure how Lee's different reasons for talking faster were going to manifest themselves. I should have just picked one of the many options Lee offered, but I feared it would result in a drawn out conversation and it was already quite late. I knew, deep down, if he just talked fast, whatever motivation he came up with would be fine with me.

The rehearsal dragged on until almost 2 AM. Since we had a 9 AM meeting at Warner Bros., I decided sleep was going to be more useful to Lee than trying to get him to talk like he was in a Preston Sturges or Howard Hawks comedy. He never got to a place close to what I was hoping for. I didn't look forward to the casting sessions in the morning. And if I might say just one more thing:

His last name is *PACE*!

We were called into Peter Roth's large office on the Warner Bros.' lot. Lee read the scene with Cami.

He was *brilliant!*

He read the two scenes we rehearsed as if on super-fast forward. Lightning fast. Somehow, in his sleep, the synapses realigned and created a superhighway. The autobahn on steroids. Everyone knew Lee was our Ned. The same thing happened at ABC. McPhearson was blown away.

To this day, watching the pilot episode of *Pushing Daisies*, I am amazed at how quickly Lee talks. I'm very proud of him.

Lee Pace catching air. Raspberry Patch, Telluride, Colorado.

Table Reads

Table reads are like a conversation with Sweetie after a dinner party when she lists all the inappropriate things I said earlier in the evening. I don't look forward to the critique, it's painful, but at the end of the day I learn a thing or two. Rarely, but occasionally, it can be fun.

A table read is when the studio, actors, writers, producers, and director hear the script read out loud by the cast for the first time. The actors sit next to each other on one side of a very long table facing an equally long table of producers, writers, studio and network execs. I warn the actors ahead of time: *talk fast*. With few exceptions table reads are nerve-wracking.

"Oh my God, this script is horrible," is the usual takeaway.

In the case of *Pushing Daisies*, most of our actors were used to network table reads and understood that this wasn't the time to try things out, discover who their character was, or talk slowly. The true purpose of a network table read, in addition to hearing if we have script issues, is that it's *another audition*. Actors sometimes get replaced after a table read . . . and that's what ABC wanted to do with Anna Friel.

As an aside: I've done four movies with Will Smith. If I ever do a fifth, I won't have him at the table read. Will's theory is he doesn't want his performance judged this early in the process. He goes out of his way to give *NO* performance. His stand-in would do a better job. It ruins the process and makes the studio think they've made a big mistake green lighting our film.

Conversely, at the table read for *Wild Wild West*, Kenneth Branagh arrived in full wardrobe and makeup—he had someone design that very cool trident facial hair he wore in the movie. He was also off book, which meant he had memorized all his lines, which is *so* British, and performed them with his character's Southern drawl. He was so good, and so totally immersed in the character, that Lorenzo di Bonaventura, the president of Warner Bros., approached me after the table read and said,

"Any way we can we fire Branagh and hire *that* guy?"

"Branagh *is* that guy," I replied.

I've rarely attended a perfect table read.

A week before we started filming the musical *Schmigadoon!* for Apple TV+ our cast came together in the Hilton Metrotown ballroom, just outside of Vancouver. Over the course of multiple hours, they read the six very funny scripts. As always, there was an endless row of actors facing an endless row of producers, crew members, writers, and me. Due to Covid, the studio executives were back in LA watching on Zoom, which was fine with me. Kristin Chenoweth, having memorized her four-minute tour de force, "Tribulation," garnered a standing ovation.

On the other hand, the table read for *Pushing Daisies* took place in a low-ceilinged florescent lit conference room at ABC in Burbank. Anna Friel was more from the Will Smith school of table reading. Not that she didn't want to be judged, just that she didn't know her character yet, and wasn't acting the part so much as reading it.

After the read through, the actors waited outside in a narrow hallway as the network and studio execs, producers, and I stayed in the room to have our postmortem.

"She's got to go," said ABC chairman Steve McPherson.

After a long discussion, based on my strong belief Anna was the right actor, and my promise I could get Anna where we needed her, Steve agreed to keep her on our show.

"You better be fucking right about this Sonnenfeld. And fix those teeth!"

If Anna hadn't already been overwhelmed and stunned by how strangely everyone treated her after the table read, she must have been particularly taken aback by the whole dental situation. Steve McPherson wanted us to cap Anna's teeth.

During the 19 days of filming the pilot episode, my main direction to Lee was to talk faster, and for Anna, it was to be happier. Anna wasn't comfortable with happy, feeling it was fake, or TV-ish. Almost daily there was a discussion about her character's emotional state.

"Anna. You can't be so glum. Be happy. Be enthusiastic."

"In other words," said Anna, "don't be real. Just be a goofy, happy, television actress."

"People can be both happy and real, Anna. In fact, in Chuck's case, she's got a second chance at life. And she's in love. Plus, she literally has been brought back from the dead. Why wouldn't she be happy?

"And also . . . talk faster."

Anna and Lee were in London the day I was in New York City for the network upfronts where television networks preview their new shows to advertisers. My cell phone rang, and it was our two leads who had just watched a screening of the pilot. They were both thrilled. Anna was giddy.

"Now will you trust my instincts?" she asked without irony.

"You mean, about not being sullen, and playing all those scenes with joy and happiness?" I responded.

"Exactly."

"Absolutely, Anna."

New Year's Eve, 2007. Telluride, Colorado.

The Experts

Not since my first job as cinematographer on *Blood Simple* had I read a script where I knew the final product was going to be special. Bryan Fuller, the writer and executive producer of *Pushing Daisies*, had created a unique, original show. I loved our collaboration.

Most people feared or hated Steve McPherson, ABC's president. Not me. I thought he was great. What made me love him was he didn't mince words.

"That sucks!" is a much better studio response to a suggestion than "Give us the weekend to think about it," which is executive-speak for "that sucks," with the downside being you have to wait a weekend to be given the bad news.

I once directed a TV comedy pilot that had a lousy table read. The writers, producers, and network president, along with his "creative staff," spent an hour debating how to improve the script. There were discussions about motivation, emotion, relationships . . .

After an hour of me sitting silently [not easy], I asked:

"What if we disregarded everything we've been talking about and just made it funnier?"

"Even better," replied the president of the network.

One area of production all executives think they're experts in is wardrobe. Never, ever, show bad wardrobe to studio executives.

Once they believe you've gone in a wrong direction, dailies are scrutinized exclusively for wardrobe.

Before the start of a movie or TV show there's a dreaded "Tone Meeting." In the case of *Pushing Daisies*, this meant presenting Steve McPherson and his "creative executives" with a book of photos and illustrations of the locations, sets, key props, and dreaded wardrobe.

The night before our meeting with McPherson I removed the wardrobe photos from the tone book.

"McPherson is going to go nuts," the producers worried. "You can't do that," warned Bruce Cohen.

"Better he sees no wardrobe than bad wardrobe. I'll just tell Steve the truth—that we're still working on it. Show an executive bad costumes and you know what happens," I countered.

"As long as he screams at you and not us," Dan Jinks bravely announced.

The next morning, I stood behind the seated McPherson and his "creative team" so I could reach past them and turn pages of the tone book fast enough to not let them dwell on minutiae. Steve was loving what he was seeing. The sets, designed by Michael Wylie, were beautiful.

I finished turning the pages and closed the book.

"Where's the fucking wardrobe?" Steve thundered.

"We're not ready to show it, Steve," I calmly said.

"OK. Great work fellas."

And there's a lesson for budding filmmakers.

There are two other areas where studio executives are self-appointed experts: visual effects and music. Luckily these two categories come after the film is shot, so there's less they can do to permanently screw things up.

No matter how many times you tell studio executives that the rough cut they are about to watch has temporary music and temporary visual effects, 90 percent of the notes you'll receive after they view your edit are about the temporary music and visual effects.

I like to start shooting a TV show or movie on the last day of preproduction. I call it "Day Zero." The crew is ready, the sets are done, wardrobe chosen, we have the film equipment, and the actors are all available, so I start filming. It's like a free day. We tell the studio we're just shooting some last-minute tests, and no one is the wiser.

On *Pushing Daisies* the crew spent Day Zero at Brown Ranch, an hour or two north of Los Angeles. I warned Peter Roth, chairman of Warner Bros. TV, he was going to see some "test" dailies the next day, and not to worry that the brown hill had no daisies. It was a "test" [it wasn't] and the brown hill would eventually be a riot of daisies [it would be].

Two days later, after viewing the "test," I received a call from Peter Roth:

"What the fuck are you doing? The show is called *Pushing Daisies*, and you've got a brown hill with a half dozen flowerpots with daisies in them? That's your field of daisies?"

"Hey Peter. Remember I said you'd be seeing a 'test' of a brown hill that would eventually, with visual effects, be covered in daisies?"

"You told me that. But then I looked at those dailies and I saw those stupid flowerpots! That's not a hill of daisies."

"Right. The flowerpots of daisies were put there so the VFX team has a reference as to color and size and perspective for when the brown hill is replaced with daisies."

"You never mentioned flowerpots!"

What's really discomforting is that Peter Roth was one of the smartest people running a movie or television studio.

Pushing Daisies was a mid-season replacement that got good reviews and was increasing its audience when the season ended. Then there was a writers' strike. By the time we were back on the air for a truncated second season it was close to a year later, and we never gained momentum. It's a shame because we had a unique premise, a wonderful creator/show runner, and an amazing cast that not only included Lee and Anna, but also Kristin Chenoweth, Chi McBride, Swoosie Kurtz, and the needy but talented Ellen Greene. A missed opportunity.

I won an Emmy for directing the pilot of *Pushing Daisies*. My acceptance speech ended with the following prescient warning:

"Love Television.

"Fear the Internet."

The Unbearable Slog of Massive Stupidity

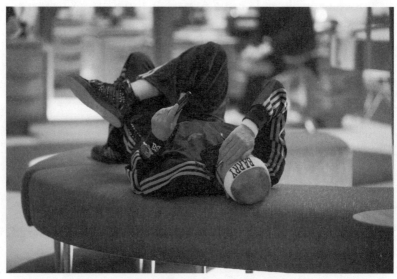

Directing Men in Black 3. *Outfit and sweatband a birthday present from Will Smith.*

started getting cryptic calls months before an official offer. Mike Simpson, my agent, and Melanie Cook, my lawyer, asked if I would consider directing *Men in Black 3* if an offer came my way.

Amy Pascal was going through a box office dry spell and her board was impatient. Her two golden ticket IPs were the Spider-Man and Men in Black franchises. Pascal needed a third *Men in Black* in a big way. It had been eight years since the release of *Men in Black II*. Amy asked Walter Parkes, who was still running Spielberg's company, to develop a script.

The movie became less theoretical when Walter called and asked if we could meet at The Odeon, a French bistro in Tribeca. I had steak au poivre with frites and an iced tea. Profiteroles for dessert.

The plot for the third movie was based on Will Smith's idea from years earlier, pitched late one night on the set of *Men in Black II*:

"I arrive back at MIB Headquarters, and it's destroyed. Tommy is gone and nobody at MIB knows who I am. I realize that a villain that Tommy had put away years earlier has escaped prison, traveled back in time 20 or 30 years, and killed Tommy. Now that Tommy is dead, everything in modern times has been changed, which is why the villain was able to destroy the headquarters, and the reason that no one knows who I am, since Tommy never recruited me. I have to travel back in time to prevent Tommy from being murdered. I see my widower father killed while he saves Tommy. Tommy shoots and kills the time traveling villain, rescues young me, who is like six at the time, and then neuralyzes me. The audience realizes that Tommy has probably erased my memory many times over the years and in fact has raised me, and it was no accident he recruited me."

Brilliant pitch, Mr. Smith!

Walter explained he had hired writer Etan Cohen, and SONY was on board with the plot. Was I interested?

As always with Walter, we were in sync when food was involved, and The Odeon is a fine French bistro. So sure. I'm in.

There were several reasons Amy thought Will's idea was great for *MIB3*. First, time travel was an original story for the franchise. Even more important, since most of the film took place in the past—with another actor playing young Tommy Lee Jones—it saved SONY many millions of dollars. Will and Tommy had contractual parity. Whatever Will was paid, so was Tommy. Add to that large number whatever Parkes/McDonald and Spielberg were raking in, and we're talking about serious money. This new script would allow SONY to pay Tommy a flat fee for ten days of work. That cost, plus the salary for young Agent K, eventually played by Josh Brolin, would be substantially less than paying Tommy parity with Will.

For his two weeks of work, Mr. Jones negotiated ten times more in salary than the studio thought they'd have to cough up. Tommy also negotiated punishing fees for every day over the ten in his contract.

One of the more surreal franchise moments occurred when Walter, Laurie, and I flew down to meet TLJ and his lovely wife, Dawn, at Tommy's polo club in West Palm Beach. Dawn was an excellent camera assistant on an earlier *Men in Black*, where TLJ and she first met.

Dawn and Tommy. West Palm Beach, 2010.

I had enjoyed watching the mating ritual between Tommy and Dawn on set. Dawn would head over to the camera cart to pick up two heavy metal cases of 35mm film, each weighing about 30 pounds. Tommy, like a golden retriever puppy desperate to please his potential new friend, would shoot out of his chair, heading towards the cases of film.

"Can I bring these somewhere for you, Dawn?"

"Put the damn cases down, Mr. Jones!" Dawn would growl.

Adorable.

Tommy was quite upset with the script for *Men in Black 3*. He had been given no warning, no heartfelt phone call from a producer with silver hair, before reading the script that dumped him from the franchise he helped create. Now we were meeting him to make nice.

"This is hard for me to take. I don't want to see another actor playing my part. Josh Brolin is a good man. I like him. He's a good actor. But do you really want to do this to the franchise? Do you really want to do this to me? Why would I want to be a party to this? I love Will and Barry and I think they feel the same about me. Why did this happen?" Tommy asked Walter.

Walter's response was not helpful:

"You know, Tommy. I'm going to err on the side of honesty."

Walter then lied to TLJ, but that's beside the point. Once Walter was done with his gobbledygook, I told Tommy he was being written out for financial reasons. Tommy got his revenge a year later. After a couple of test screenings, SONY decided we needed an additional ending, requiring the return of Agent K. Those two additional days of non-contractual filming were very lucrative for Mr. Jones.

Amy, for a third consecutive time working with her, backed into a release date, this time summer 2012. She decided the film would start preproduction in Los Angeles at the beginning of 2010, but film exclusively in New York City. I thought this was a bad idea. The majority of the first two *MIBs* were shot in LA on the SONY lot, each movie spending less than a month filming exteriors in New York. I had a sense that Will wanted to be close to home in Los Angeles, and I wasn't wrong.

Building the many sets on the SONY stages in LA would have also consolidated our footprint, allowing me to efficiently walk to a different stage to set up second unit shots or quickly give my opinion about ongoing set construction. In New York, we were trifurcated between the Marcy Avenue Armory in Williamsburg, Brooklyn, where we built Men in Black Headquarters; the stages at Kaufman Astoria Studios in Queens where we constructed several sets including the Cape Canaveral launch pad and Wu's Chinese restaurant; and finally, Steiner Studios near the Brooklyn shipyards where the LunaMax prison and the top of the Chrysler Building were located.

The fable about a scorpion and a frog—"You knew I was a scorpion when you gave me a ride"—describes Walter and my relationship. After I made my deal to direct *MIB3*, he refused to hire Graham Place, my good friend and producer of the first two *MIBs*, to cut off my support. The bickering only escalated from there.

Early on, Amy and SONY's marketing team asked if I could find a scene that could take place at a Radio Shack, which was willing to spend millions of dollars for a huge co-branded advertising campaign. I suggested the movie's time travel device could be hidden at a Radio Shack. The "Shack" was the lowest of the low-tech electronics stores, making it very *on tone* that the most advanced piece of electronics in the universe was hidden in the most mundane place.

In addition to a massive advertising spend, Radio Shack agreed to finance the construction of a Radio Shack store on stage. This not only saved us a day of shooting on location, it also saved us a location fee, plus we could pre-light the set and film the scene in a half day.

After the legalities were worked out, Walter announced he hated it. Product placement with Radio Shack seemed like a loser move and he would not allow it.

Suddenly, Amy didn't like the idea either. The deal was killed.

Agent J on top of the Chrysler Building set. Steiner Studios.

What a Director Needs

I buried the lede. All of these issues were minor compared to the real idiocy:

In an act of expensive lunacy, SONY insisted we begin shooting *MIB3* with only one-third of a script. Amy Pascal and Walter Parkes' plan was to continue the writing process while filming the first act. Absent a finished script, we'd stop filming for several months, keeping everyone on salary and paying to hold our stages in New York, while more of the movie was written and prepped. In a perfect world Walter and Etan would finish the entire script, but if not, we'd shut down a second time while the final third of the script was written. Which is what happened.

The tail wagging the dog aspect of this was Amy's need to announce a big movie with a summer 2012 release date. She was panicked due to the rumor Mr. Summer Blockbuster was circling a movie at Warner Bros., which would tie him up for six months. Concerned for her job security, she feared if Will took the Warner's gig, she wouldn't be able to back into that summer 2012 release date.

Will and I begged Amy not to go forward with this dumb, irresponsible plan. Will promised he'd be available for *MIB3* as soon as there was a finished script. I reminded Amy she had years earlier admitted her error backing into a release date for *Men in Black II*, and how she had vowed to never make that mistake again.

I constantly pleaded that a director needs an entire script before starting to shoot since comedy callbacks, visual callbacks, setting up pace and structure, pretty much everything involved in the creative process of directing a movie, requires an entire script. I employed metaphors like building a house, or designing a car without having all the necessary blueprints, but I got a lot of:

"Yes, Barry. We know what a director needs and you're going to have to deal with not having what you need."

On a Friday evening a week before the start of principal photography, Walter, Laurie, Amy, and Doug Belgrad showed up at the Armory to examine our new MIB Headquarters set for the first time.

What I thought was going to be a cursory tour, a visual victory lap for Bo Welch and me, was a disaster. I was barely able to walk by the time my sciatica-inducing visitors departed. The first scene in the new headquarters involved a memorial for the recently departed Zed. The eulogy, given by Agent K, as well as a speech in an alien language by Emma Thompson [Agent O], took place in front of a series of pedestals with identical crystal busts of fallen MIB heroes. The location of these pedestals was against a far wall of the set, quite a distance from the public area where aliens congregate.

Walter went ballistic.

Tommy Lee Jones. Men in Black Headquarters memorial.

"We can't have these busts out in the open where visiting aliens could see which agents are dead! They need to rise out of the floor. This is a total disaster."

"We're showing a bunch of identical busts. We'll never see them after this scene. There'll never be a shot connecting visiting aliens and the memorial. Plus, we come onto the scene in progress, so who knows if the busts are always in view," I implored. "The audience has no idea where the memorial is located within the headquarters. And the only aliens in the scene are invited dignitaries that knew Zed."

"The pedestals have to rise up from the floor, then disappear at the end of the scene. And the audience needs to see it happening. Arriving aliens can never know about the memorial. There's no other solution," lectured Walter.

"There are no arriving aliens in the scene, Walter."

And . . . Amy, not wanting to ruffle feathers unless they were mine, agreed with Walter. The pedestals had to start under the floor and via visual effects, rise on cue, adding significant computer graphics costs. I took Belgrad, always a voice of reason, off to the side and complained it was nuts to spend additional money to placate Walter.

"We're talking about way more than a hundred thousand dollars for something we don't need," I pleaded.

"Just do it," offered the wise Belgrad. "It isn't your money."

Weird Technique

As much as I wanted Josh Brolin to play young Agent K, that's how much Ari Emanuel, chairman of William Morris Endeavor talent agency, wanted the part for Mark Wahlberg. What's fascinating is all three of us—Brolin, Wahlberg, and Sonnenfeld—were clients of WME. In fact, Josh and Mark were both represented personally by the chairman.

Ari had a unique telephone technique that somehow in his mind made him super-duper powerful. I was familiar with the Scott Rudin phone concept, whereby assistants rolled hundreds of calls a day leaving messages just so you'd always have Rudin on your mind. Occasionally a Rudin assistant would accidentally call when you were available, in which case the assistant would say they just lost him, he'll call back.

Ari had a whole different style.

"Hello," I spoke into my cell phone.

"Can you hold for Ari Emanuel?"

"Sure."

Ari would wait long enough to become annoying, and at the point I assumed the call had been dropped, he would pick up.

"What?"

"Excuse me?"

"I'm returning your call."

"I didn't call you, Ari."

"Yes you did. I'm returning your call."

"Must be another Barry. Levinson?"

"Sonnenfeld. I am returning your call."

"Ari, I swear, I did not call you."

"Yes you did."

"OK. Well, um, whatever I called you about, I guess I can't remember. Sorry to waste your time. See ya."

"Wait. Sonnenfeld. Since we're on the phone anyway, what about Wahlberg for the young Tommy Lee Jones part?"

"We're out to Brolin. You represent him."

"Are you going to be in New York soon? Mark would love to meet you."

"Ari. We're out to *your* client. Josh Brolin."

"You're making a mistake, Sonnenfeld."

"Got it. Thanks, Ari."

A week later my phone rang.

"Please hold for Ari Emanuel."

After an endless delay, Ari, sounding annoyed, asked:

"What?"

"Huh?"

"What do you want, Sonnenfeld?"

"Um . . . I don't want anything."

"You called me. You want something."

"Ari. I swear. I have never, ever, in my life called you."

"Yes you did. I'm returning your call. From earlier."

"OK, well, in any case, I'm sorry but I forgot why I called. And Ari. Assume any time anyone tells you I called, I didn't. See ya."

"Wait. Since we're on the phone . . . I talked to Walter and he says you'll be in New York next week casting, so I've set up a time for you and Walter and Laurie to meet Wahlberg. You're going to love him."

"What about Josh, Ari?"

"Meet Wahlberg. Then we can discuss Josh."

"Hey, Ari. Just so you know. I didn't call you. Like . . . *EVER*."

"Yes you did," Ari barked, trying to get in his last "Tag. You're it," as he raced to hang up.

Walter, Laurie, and I met Wahlberg. He was charming and smart, and he was a great second choice. I hope to work with him some day.

Josh eventually signed on to the role after Ari ran out of reasons not to hire him. Soon after we started production, Brolin left WME.

Faster. Flatter. Part 2

I met Michael Stuhlbarg at Bubby's, a hip Tribeca diner famous for their pancakes and pies. We were there to discuss the role of Griffin the Archanan in *Men in Black 3*. Stuhlbarg was lovely, smart, and intense. Every word I uttered seemed fascinating to him. He also took a great deal of time studying the menu as if this laminated sheet of bleached and processed wood pulp that listed prepared food items for sale was unique to Bubby's.

It felt like I was having a discussion with an alien who could pass as human, which was, by the way, exactly the role, so it was a bit of typecasting.

Why hire an actor to play an alien when I can get this actual alien to play an alien?

I offered him the part.

As days became weeks and started to become months, I could not get an answer from Michael. I was running out of time and patience and called his agent, the smart and lovely Hildy Gottlieb.

"Hey, Hildy. What's going on with Michael? He's either got to commit or I have to move on. I'm running out of time."

Hildy explained, "Michael views himself as 'a serious actor' and needs to wrap his head around a role before he can commit. He needs to live in the part, feel if it's him."

"I get that Hildy but let him know he's either got to stop wrapping his head, or I've got to find a 'less serious' actor. Besides. Why would he even want to wrap his human head inside an alien that lives in trillions of multiverses simultaneously? It seems kinda daunting."

"Let me see what I can do," Hildy promised.

As soon as Michael committed, I got a call from a director friend of mine.

"You're going to hate working with him," he told me.

"Why's that?"

"He'll never talk fast enough. I tried for an entire movie. I told him he thinks he's controlling his screen time, talking so slowly that I'm stuck on his shot, but I explained it was just the opposite. By talking slowly I'm forced to cut away from him to speed up his off-camera dialogue."

"I can get anyone to talk fast," I bragged.

Once we started shooting *MIB3* I was proven so, so wrong.

I could not get Michael to speed up his performance.

"Cut. Great. Let's do another one, but Michael, talk like WAY faster."

"You got it, Barry," he would say.

"Cut. Great. Let's do another one, but Michael . . . like a billion times faster. Literally. A billion times."

I'm not sure he actually thought he was talking faster, but his performance was like verbal taffy.

I rarely give actors backstories or acting motivation for why they should change a performance. As I told Lee Pace on *Pushing Daisies* when he asked if I wanted him to talk faster because his character was hiding something, or devious, or nervous:

"Just talk faster."

On the first *Men in Black*, I had a discussion with Vincent D'Onofrio on what it was like being directed by Stanley Kubrick, my favorite filmmaker. Vincent was brilliant in *Full Metal Jacket*, so I was interested to know how a real director talks to actors.

"Stanley had me come to London months before we started filming," said D'Onofrio. "Once a week we'd meet at his estate, he'd look me over, and say, 'Gain more weight.'

"After *a lot* of weeks of pretty much doing nothing but eating, Stanley gave me the once over and said: 'Good.'

"I was finally obese enough, and I assumed we could finally talk about my character.

"'Stanley, at the beginning of the movie, when I first . . .'

"'You're the actor. Figure it out. That's *your* job, not mine.'

"And that was the last time we talked about performance," Vincent said.

But I'm not Kubrick. And Michael Stuhlbarg wasn't saying his lines fast enough.

We were on the set of Andy Warhol's loft, called The Factory. There were scores of extras, Bill Hader was playing Andy Warhol [and Agent W], and tonally, the scene was a tightrope walk between comedy and action, which is always a challenge. In addition, this scene was the audience's introduction to the aforementioned Griffin the Archanan, Michael's character.

Bill Hader getting final touch-ups by Rick Baker
on the right side of frame.

The scene set up Griffin's ability to see every possible iteration of the future in real time. We also needed to reveal Griffin was an alien who passed as a human. The reason he's wearing a wool hat and multiple layers of outerwear in the middle of summer is because 90 degrees Fahrenheit on his planet is brutally cold.

I sadly realized I was going to have to pretend I was a "real director" and talk to a "real actor," because saying "talk faster" wasn't working.

"Hey, Michael."

"Yes, Barry."

"You know how your character, Griffin the Archanan, is like a Quantum Mechanic?"

"Yes. That's who I am. I am Griffin the Archanan, the Quantum Mechanic."

"So, the thing about you being a Quantum Mechanic, is that you see all possibilities of every situation. All possible outcomes. A sneeze, cough, trip, laugh, fall . . . an additional word, missing an elevator. . . . Anything that happens can change the outcome of everything that follows, every instant of every day. That's billions of trillions of possibilities every second, right?"

"Absolutely."

"Every instant, everyone in this room, in this city, in this country, on Earth, every decision each and everyone makes, changes everything. Griffin knows someone leaving this party two seconds later will mean they get hit by a bus a week from Tuesday, because of all the events between now and then which have changed, just because they left this party a couple of seconds late. All the billions upon trillions of computations that each and every person's decisions force you to calculate."

"Yes!"

"And that's why Griffin the Archanan, the Quantum Mechanic, has to talk incredibly fast. Because he knows by the time he reaches the end of his sentence, if he isn't talking fast enough, whatever he's talking about can change. All these intertwined interactions can screw up what Griffin is referencing before he finishes his thought. Unless . . . "

"He talks really fast!" Stuhlbarg realizes.

"That's right," I say.

"Got it!" Michael gleefully shouts. "Let's go!"

And for the rest of the show, he spoke incredibly fast.

Me and Michael: Andy Warhol's loft. MIB3.

She's Greek

We were filming a funny scene in MIB Headquarters between Will Smith and the young 1969 version of Agent K, played, despite Ari Emanuel, by Josh Brolin. Mike Soccio, a member of Will's writing team, had come up with a funny ad-lib for Will while being interrogated by Brolin.

"What's your girlfriend's name?"

"Sssttarrran," Will stutters his answer after much hesitation.

"Sssttarrran?" Brolin incredulously responds.

"Yeah. She's ah . . . . Greek," ad-libs Will.

Minutes before flinging a chair across MIB Headquarters: "Yeah. She's Greek."

If you are a studio executive on set that day, and don't like this very funny ad-lib, or you're afraid Walter won't like it, you might ask yourself: "Is Barry covering this dialogue in other angles besides the wide master?"

Absolutely. There is so much coverage you can cut out anything that isn't working.

Unfortunately, Jonathan Kadin, the SONY executive assigned to our show, made the mistake of school teaching me, saying I wasn't allowed to shoot anything not in the script. News to me.

"You have to do a take where Will doesn't improv that line," Kadin demanded.

I went ballistic. The week had been particularly stressful, and this latest dumb obstacle was too much. I grabbed one of those tall director's chairs and flung it.

"Are you nuts?" I screamed at Jonathan. "Do you know so little about how films are made you don't realize the really funny ad-lib can be cut out in editorial? *AND* show me the rule that says I can't shoot anything not in the script.

"Leave.

"Now."

For the first time in probably 15 years, I lost my cool and yelled at someone on set. Although it briefly reduced my sciatica, that joyful pain-free status only lasted an hour or two.

Kadin grabbed his belongings and slumped his way out of the armory and into the moist, clammy summer evening air of Williamsburg, dodging Orthodox Jews on the way to shul, each zealot wearing a mink hat the size of a baby goat sitting on a bundt pan.

I apologized to Gary Martin, who was on set that day, for throwing a chair. Gary's response:

"I don't have any problem with you throwing chairs. But next time don't throw mine."

"At least you weren't sitting in it, Gar," I smiled.

The Wrong City

Although Will never demanded it [and I wish he had], from the beginning of *Men in Black 3*'s inception, I sensed he wanted to use the same shooting template as the first two movies; spend a few weeks in New York filming exteriors, then move the majority of the shoot to stages in Los Angeles. Once SONY insisted on an all New York shoot, Will used everything in his massive power to get back to LA as often as possible. At first, he requested changes to the shooting schedule so he could have a Friday or Monday off. Then it became a Friday *and* Monday. Then it was midday Thursday instead of Friday morning. I tried to give him as much time as he asked for.

Will and me on his studio apartment set. Men in Black 3.

I wasn't working with the Will Smith I knew. He was mopey, slightly testy to his hair and makeup crew, and even when the camera was rolling, I had to remind him that Agent K was the sourpuss and Agent J was the upbeat guy. He was really suffering. About three-quarters of the way through the shoot, at 10 AM on a Tuesday morning, Will took me aside and dropped the following into my director's lap:

"So, Baz: I'm here for another two hours. Then I'm heading to Teterboro [an airport in New Jersey that catered to private planes] and heading home. That's where I need to be. I have to be with Jada. I'll be back for Monday's work. And one other thing, Baz: This has to be your idea. You want me to take the rest of the week off. This isn't something I'm asking for. This is something you want me to have. This is all on you."

"Can Jada come here instead?"

"Nope."

"You're scheduled in every scene from today through Friday. It's going to be impossible to fill three and a half full days of work that doesn't include you. And what am I supposed to tell people? Why am I giving you three and a half days off?"

"Figure it out, Baz. You're the director. I'm on that plane in two hours."

Michael Lerman was an excellent first assistant director. Although his resting face implied his dog just died, it was clever camouflage for his sardonic wit and go-to attitude. Lerman had put up with constant changing schedules as various scenes and sets were built, dropped from the script, then put back in again. He had to schedule a film where half the script hadn't been written and keep each day's work moving efficiently. But this was about to be a bridge too far.

"So, Michael, we need to talk," I said.

"What's up, boss?"

"I've decided to give Will the rest of the week off. He's tired and needs to recuperate back in LA."

"What?!" Lerman shot at me. "You can't be serious. Will's in every scene."

"Yeah, I know. So let's figure out what we can slot into the schedule for the next several days, OK?"

"What are you not telling me?"

"Nothing Lerman. I'm not telling you nothing."

Soon after my discussion with Lerman, and before we figured out how to cobble various pieces of scenes together, Michael wrote a mean text about me to his wife. Unfortunately, although meant for his wife, he accidentally sent it to me.

"I agree, Lerman," I whispered to him as I walked to craft services.

Lerman dreaming about his next job.

Brolin, who was never told why we were changing everything around, bore the brunt of this mess. He ended up acting in parts of scenes with off-camera me, or the off-camera script supervisor. It wasn't fair to Josh, and he kind of gave up on our show at that point. By the end of filming, Josh wasn't talking to me, and I don't blame him.

Old School

It is 8 PM and we're on the Men in Black Headquarters set. I'm sitting on my saddle looking at Will, whose learning his lines for a new scene Walter Parkes has sent to set. Will had not yet kicked Walter off the movie, so we are still receiving new scenes from Parkes.

Director and saddle. MIB Headquarters. Tam and scarf courtesy of Emma Thompson.

"Hey, Walter. Can I talk to you about some of this dialogue?"

Walter is off set, so this conversation with the producer is taking place over the phone.

"I'm in the middle of dinner, Barry."

"Right. But we're about to shoot this scene, and . . . "

"I just got off the phone with Amy. She's read the pages, loves them, and says don't change a word," orders Walter.

Amy, of course, doesn't answer her cell phone so I don't know if Walter is telling the truth about her loving the pages or if in fact, she's even seen them. At this point, communication on the show is so dysfunctional I have no choice but to shoot now and ask questions later. I pick up my phone to call Sweetie and tell her I'll be home late, that Walter has some lame new pages he wants me to shoot. As I pick up my iPhone, Jada's brother Caleeb, who Will has made his script doctor, is standing over my shoulder, looking at my screen, which is a beautiful photo of Sweetie with a stylish short haircut, from a decade earlier. As Will lifts a paper cup of coffee to his mouth [Will is not a coffee drinker but it's late and we're confused], Will and I hear Caleeb say:

"Old school. Michael J. Fox. Love it."

Screen saver. Sweetie, 2002.

In a totally flat unemotional voice, I say:

"That's my wife."

Will Smith does a Danny Thomas spit take and spews coffee over my face, shirt, jacket, and Caleeb. To this day, Caleeb blushes when he sees me.

At the end of the evening, Walter came back to set as we were packing up for the night and asked how it went.

"Just fine, Walter."

"Ya want to hear something, Barry."

"Sure, Walter."

"The pages—you say they were fine. Right?"

"Yes, Walter. I say they were fine."

"Well, here's what you didn't know. I wrote them!"

I had assumed this, since there were no writers on the show at the moment and there was a certain unsubtle exposition to the writing that hinted at Walter's métier.

"And they're good, right?"

"They're fine."

"You see, Ba. Here's the problem with my job," Walter continued. "Let's say this show is a massive critical and box office success."

"Unlikely, Walter, but go ahead."

"Let's just say."

"Sure."

"Huge critical success."

"Goes without saying."

"You get to go up on stage and accept the Oscar for directing. Will gets one for acting."

"Sure."

"What's my reward? I get to go up and accept the Oscar for best picture? Who cares? What's the upside in that? I want to be on stage receiving the award for WRITING. That's what it's about! Isn't it?"

"So, Walter. You'd rather be known as the Oscar winning writer of a movie than the producer of the best picture of the year."

"Absolutely. There's nothing in it for me to be the producer of the best movie. It's all about the writing."

That discussion explains everything that was wrong with the most dysfunctional successful franchise in movie history. It had no producer.

Chocolate Milk

David Koepp had been hired twice to rewrite *Men in Black 3*. The talented Etan Cohen, who wrote the original draft, was fired and rehired three or four times before we were done.

There were other writers. Academy Award winning screenwriter Michael Arndt, of *Little Miss Sunshine*, was on board for a couple of weeks, as was Jeff Nathanson, who wrote *The Terminal* for Walter and Laurie.

One of Koepp's talents is writing comedy within action—almost an oxymoron. Action kills comedy—and comedy, requiring setups and punchlines, usually makes the action look ridiculous as actors delay their action in service to a funny line. Koepp is one of the few writers to pull off the near impossibility of writing action and comedy in the same scene.

Add in the difficulties of writing within a time travel plot and you've got some major challenges.

Dave and I felt we needed a specific action that made Agent O, Emma Thompson's character, realize that Agent J had become "enmeshed" in a time travel incident. Koepp's solution was that a couple of times early in the film, Agent J should crave chocolate milk, which we learn can be associated with time travel. Specific. Funny. And on plot. There were two pivotal scenes where we set this up.

In the first, Agent J, freaked out because Agent K has disappeared and no one at MIB Headquarters remembers K, heads over to his partner's apartment. He knocks on the door and is shocked when it is answered by a mother holding a baby. The mother was played by my stepdaughter, Sasha, and the toddler, with a sippy cup of chocolate milk, was played by her daughter, Violet.

Before leaving, Will takes the cup of chocolate milk from the kid and downs it.

Will came up with a funny ad-lib for Violet, which was:

"Mommy. The president is drinking my chocolate milk." [Obama was POTUS at the time.]

The second scene that reinforces his time travel enmeshment is at MIB Headquarters where Agent O discovers that Agent J is craving "chocolatized dairy products." She knows that desiring chocolate milk can be an indication of someone, somehow, being entangled in a time travel event. Easy to follow for the audience and a very specific setup to the plot.

Walter hated it. He thought the chocolate milk MacGuffin was too specific [a MacGuffin is a plot device used to attract the audience's attention but isn't necessarily important to the story]. My feeling was in a time travel movie the more clues you give an audience, the easier it is for them to follow the plot.

The morning we were scheduled to film Agent J showing up to Agent K's apartment, we had still not resolved if the chocolate milk reference would be used. Will and I wanted it. Walter and Laurie didn't.

Walter declared under no circumstances would he allow me to shoot the chocolate milk version. Of course, that was the one day on the entire show Steven Spielberg, the most powerful man in show biz and a producer on the movie, whose ear was close to

Walter's mouth, was visiting the set. I left the stage, crossed the street to Will's double decker camper, and told him Walter refused to let me shoot the chocolate milk version. Despite Walter's threat, and Spielberg's arrival, I would film it both ways. With and without chocolate milk.

Will refused.

"You're the director, Baz. I'm going to do it one way only. What do *you* want because that's the only version I'll do."

Oy.

We were lit and ready to film the scene. I called Will, Sasha, and Violet to the stage. Sitting in video village, on director's chairs, were Walter, Laurie, and Steven Spielberg. I sat on my saddle next to the camera inside the set far away from the three producers.

Our first shot was over Will's shoulder onto Sasha and Violet, who, as per my instruction, had a sippy cup in her hand half filled with chocolate milk. We did a couple of takes. Will drank the chocolatized dairy product.

I was happy with the acting and announced we were moving on to another angle of the scene.

Lerhman, the often depressed looking first assistant director, tells me Steven is asking if he could have a word. I amble off my saddle, leave the set, and sit next to Mr. Spielberg on a director's chair.

"Hey, Barry. What's up with the chocolate milk?"

Walter had gotten to him.

Steven Spielberg and I debate chocolate milk.

"It is a very specific action—craving chocolate milk. It's the setup for the next scene at MIB Headquarters. Emma hears Will demanding chocolate milk. She knows when someone is craving 'chocolatized dairy products' there's a chance it is due to time travel. It is specific and Koepp did a great job writing it."

"Can we do a take without it?"

"Well, Steven, Will says he won't do two versions of the scene, so if you feel strongly about it, you'll have to talk to him yourself, since I like the chocolate milk scene, and Will agrees."

"Got it. Thanks, Barry."

I was impressed that Steven did not force the issue. I suspect several reasons:

I think he knew Will and I were right—its specificity helped tell the story.

I also think Steven's instinct, unlike Walter's, was to trust me.

And, finally, who in God's name wants to confront a very powerful actor? Not even Steven Spielberg.

Why Are We Here Mel? Part 2

No one said the obvious part out loud. Why are we making multiple scouting trips to Cape Canaveral, Florida? Do we actually think we're going to shoot the ending of our show on the real launch gantry hundreds of feet in the air? It was a bonkers idea and took way too long to realize just how wacky a concept it was. The logistics of bringing all our camera, grip, and electric equipment up in one elevator, then rigging the lights and putting the actors in safety harnesses was insane. Then there was also the time suck of having to get on the single elevator to take you back down the 370 feet to sea level for a quick bathroom break.

In addition, the launch tower for the space shuttle looks *nothing like* the Saturn V tower used for the 1969 moon launch. We would have to make so many modifications using computer graphics in editing that the actual tower was useless.

2004 vs. 1969.

On the other hand, since we only had a partial first act, and only a vague outline for the rest of the story, we didn't have a lot of locations to obsess over. The multiple trips to the Cape allowed us to pretend we had a plan.

I did get to ride a Ritz-Carlton elevator with the always confused looking Tom Coughlin, at the time the New York Giants' head coach, so the trips weren't all for nothing.

At the end of our third excursion to the Cape [March, August, and the following March], each time scouting without a finished script, Ken Ralston, the patient and talented visual effects supervisor, Bo Welsh, Bill Pope the DP, and I got together at the Ritz bar.

"Am I missing something, or are we in the wrong place?" I asked my compatriots.

"We are *so* in the wrong place," all three chimed in.

Even Walter agreed the real Cape Canaveral was a mistake. We ended up constructing part of the tower and gantry on the big stage at Astoria Studios in Queens, and filmed the ground level base of the launch tower at Jones Beach on Long Island.

We barely got away with the finale's fight sequence on top of the gantry. It took almost a year to agree on the plot and concomitant stunt choreography for the "climax." Our highly paid stunt coordinator had left us to work on an Angelina Jolie film before he could design an exciting fight [since there was no script, he didn't know what the fight would be], leaving us in the hands of his assistant. The sequence was prosaic and serviceable at best, though not the fault of our new stunt coordinator. An action sequence that should have had months of design, stunt rehearsals, and time to film, was compressed into days.

The emotional ending, however, shot at Jones Beach, worked wonderfully. Josh and Will were quite moving. It was especially tough for Brolin, who had to work with a young kid who couldn't keep still or hold a look. Josh was patient and charming with our young actor.

Somehow seeing this sad rusted garbage can on top of the most technologically advanced launch pad in the world was the last straw.

Mein Führer. I Can Walk.

The last line of dialogue in *Dr. Strangelove*, seconds before nuclear Armageddon, comes from Doc Strangelove himself:

"Mein Führer. I can walk!"

I've had a long battle with sciatica. Dr. John Sarno, my back doctor, now deceased, believed in most cases sciatica is caused by "unconscious narcissistic rage." The unconscious part of our brain, fearing that expressing our rage will harm a relationship, or in times of profound stress, shuts down oxygen to the sciatic nerve causing so much pain down the back of the leg you can't focus on anything but that pain, preventing you from expressing anger that might ruin your life.

My first bout was in 1990 on *The Addams Family*, produced by the stress GOAT himself, Scott Rudin. I spent the entire show in pain. After the movie was released, and with Dr. Sarno's help, I was cured for more than half a decade.

But all good things must eventually come to an end:

It was a Monday evening in 1996 and the next morning we were going to film Will Smith's introduction to Men in Black Headquarters. This involved a very complicated technocrane shot in which the camera starts on Tommy and Will riding the open Juliet balconied elevator then booms down and pulls back with our two leads as they get off the elevator and walk the length of the headquarters' lobby.

Lots of extras, visual effects, a technocrane, two stars [one of them sometimes cranky], and a working elevator: What could go wrong?

Monday at wrap, I told Peter Chesney, the guy in charge of the physical effects, how important it was for things to go smoothly the next morning. The elevator had to be ready.

"Tommy Lee Jones suffers no fools, and I don't want to look like one."

"Got it," says Chesney.

"What time are your guys coming in to make sure the elevator is totally dialed in for a ten AM shoot?"

"Eight should be fine."

"Hey, Chesney. The thing has to be tested and ready to go at ten. How 'bout coming in at six?"

"It's pretty much ready. Six is overkill."

"I was going to say four. Can we please say six? I really, really, really don't want Tommy standing around because the elevator isn't ready."

"We don't need it, but how about seven."

"OK, Chesney. Seven it is. But it has to be ready."

"You got it, sir [asshole]."

At noon the next day with Tommy Lee fucking Jones cooling his jets, we still didn't have a working elevator. I couldn't take it anymore.

Screaming across the set, I yelled at Chesney and his crew:

"I BEGGED you to come in early. I said take as early a call as you want. You promised you only needed two hours and it's been five since you guys arrived. You're killing me, Chesney. This is fucking insane."

Sweetie was on set. She lovingly pulled me aside and gave me a talking to.

"They know they messed up. They are embarrassed and trying their best. Your yelling doesn't make them work faster. All it does is make *you* the villain. Instead of feeling bad, they're now angry at you. You just look mean."

Of course, Sweetie was right. I promised I would never yell at anyone again.

Instead, I live with sciatica.

Cut to more than 15 years later:

Walter Parkes and I continued to feud.

Christmas Day was a scheduled conference call with Amy Pascal, Doug Belgrad, and Walter and Laurie. The discussion was about bringing David Koepp back for a second time. The issue was that Koepp, who called Walter a time vampire, refused to discuss what he intended to write with anyone but me. He was taking the job because of our friendship and only wanted to report to the director. Any other version and Dave wouldn't work on the film. Amy was so afraid of Walter's wrath, she offered Koepp to double his weekly rate, which was probably the highest in the industry, if he agreed to have a single conversation with Walter. Dave refused. Amy and Doug agreed to Koepp's insistence he wouldn't talk to Walter, but wanted *me* to deliver the news to Walter and Laurie on this call.

David Koepp at Walter Parkes' Tribeca apartment during his first stint rewriting MIB3.

The stress of filming *MIB3* had given me the worst bout of sciatica in my life. I was literally crawling to the actors between takes. Who knew what this phone call would lead to.

I got on the conference call in my office, located on the second floor of our East Hampton home. With everyone on the phone, I explained to Walter that Koepp was only coming on board [yet again] as a favor to me. Not only did he not want to show pages to Walter and Laurie, he didn't want to hear their ideas before he started. He was writing exclusively for me.

"Well, Barry. That's just not going to work," said Walter.

"It's the only way Dave will write on the show."

No longer holding in his three films' worth of resentment and fury, Walter spewed:

"Let's be honest here, Barry. The last ten years of your personal and professional life have been nothing short of a total disaster."

There was silence on the line. I expected Amy or Belgrad to at least offer a sing-song-y Mary Tyler Moore-y response of:

"Oh, Walter . . ."

Nothing. No one spoke up on my behalf.

"You know what, Walter?

"Fuck you."

I slammed down the phone.

Stood up.

And just like Dr. Sarno predicted, having moved my rage to the *conscious* part of my brain, I was pain free.

I ran downstairs to the kitchen where Sweetie was making lunch.

"Mein Führer. I can walk!"

Banned

The temporary end of Walter came on a Friday evening, more than halfway through filming. New pages arrived from the silver haired bard. As always, Walter said these new pages had Amy's approval and must be shot. And of course, Amy was not available to verify.

The scene took place in a car, was full of bald exposition, and only made sense if connected to some as yet unwritten scenes.

We lined up the car on our blue screen stage.

Josh Brolin was in the driver's seat, Will in the passenger's. Behind them were Bill Pope—the cinematographer—and me. Will and Josh read the scene. We were perplexed.

"So, Bill. Since I don't know where this scene takes place in the script, or what location they're driving to or from for that matter, and I'm not sure if it's day or night, is there a way to generically light this so it can fit anywhere? Day or night?"

Will turned around.

"You know what, Baz. It's been a long week. If the director and actors are handed pages they've never seen before, don't know where in the script the scene goes, what location we're coming from or going to, and are not sure if it is day or night, let's go home."

Will called Amy.

Walter was banned from the set and barred from communicating with us until postproduction, when he briefly demanded an entire separate editing crew to cut his own version of the movie. Once he found out I wasn't going to fight this stupidity [my agent sagely questioned: "Can you imagine Walter spending every day in a cutting room? Let him have it."], Walter decided it wasn't worth his time and dropped the demand.

The players: Sweetie, Will, Pascal, James Lassiter, me, Doug Belgrad having fun.

The End

The last two nights of filming underneath the FDR Drive in Lower Manhattan found everyone in a bad mood. Will was physically and emotionally exhausted, his many flights back and forth to LA, plus whatever was going on once he got there, was taking a toll. Brolin had totally given up and wasn't talking to me. Bill Pope was in a lousy mood and taking it out on the crew. We were near the summer solstice and didn't have many hours of darkness each night. Unfortunately, we were filming a very important scene. Will is about to tell Josh that if he goes to Cape Canaveral, he'll die. I had to hold our actors together and pretend this was all lots of fun. I've never had less joy finishing principal photography; we just slogged our way to a temporary, always moving finish line.

Will makes a defeated halfhearted wrap speech.

After a couple of recruited audience screenings, we all agreed we needed another scene to emotionally wrap up the movie, one that would require bringing back, at great expense, but well worth it, Tommy Lee Jones. Amy, Belgrad, and I had a new ending we all felt would work: Will Smith returns to the present with the knowledge he saved Earth, saved Agent K, and that Agent K was his surrogate father. Everything is back to normal. Present day Agents J and K meet at the same diner where Will and Josh Brolin ate pie in 1969. Griffin would be there to add both tension and comic relief. Will, now aware of the sacrifice Tommy made—adopting and raising J since he was five—thanks K for all he's done. Tommy tells Will it was an honor.

Will and Tommy were wonderfully moving.

In addition to the diner scene, there was something else I wanted to shoot. Early in the movie Agent K gives a non-emotional eulogy at MIB Headquarters for Zed, the Rip Torn character. It wasn't getting the laughs we expected, and Amy wanted it gone. I felt we needed to keep the eulogy scene to explain Zed's absence as well as set up Emma Thompson's Agent O as the new leader of the Men in Black. The reason the eulogy wasn't working, I explained, is that we hadn't set up the joke. We went right to the punchline. I wanted a scene ahead of the Zed memorial that set up Agent J worrying about how lame Agent K's speech was going to be, with K promising everyone will be moved. J asks K to run the speech by him and K insists J has nothing to worry about—people will cry. Tommy Lee Jones' lame eulogy is now set up and would get the laughs it deserved.

One of the life lessons I learned from Will and James Lassiter was to never use the word "no." Don't confront and demean an opponent. Before *MIB3*, if Amy had said "I want to lose the eulogy,"

I would have immediately gone off on a tirade about how stupid and shortsighted that idea was. Instead, thanks to Will and JL's aikido negotiating technique, I said,

"You're absolutely right, Amy. Let me reiterate your point, slightly differently." I then explained in the nicest, nonconfrontational way, why not only did I want to keep the eulogy, I wanted to shoot an *additional* scene with Will and Tommy setting it up. By not immediately putting Amy on the defensive, I won her over and was given the money to shoot that scene.

And yet . . . Even though we were tens of millions over budget, there was one more Amy moment that just baffles: She would agree to the new ending in the diner—which she herself wanted—only if I used Jay-Z and Alicia Keys' song "Empire State of Mind" in the scene. The licensing cost was somewhere north of $400,000, so the fact that she would let me shoot the diner scene *she wanted*, only if I agreed to an insanely expensive song, made me suspect this was something Walter, not Amy, demanded.

Men in Black 3 was released May 25, 2012. It grossed 654 million bucks before it ended its run, making it the most successful of the three MIBs. I recently watched the movie and was pleasantly surprised how on purpose it felt. Movie magic.

The Cat Whisperer

As a reminder, there are three bullet points for choosing a movie to direct: money, location, and script. Rarely am I able to check all three boxes. In the case of *Nine Lives*, I started with two out of three but as always hoped to make the script a lot better.

I met Christophe Lambert, the very handsome, very French and charming CEO of EuropaCorp, for lunch at Locanda Verde in New York City. He was about to convince me to direct *Nine Lives* for his French production company founded by Luc Besson. Christophe would produce.

Directing a movie about a cat would be problematic since I am *highly* allergic. I can get in a New York taxi and know that within the past 48 hours a passenger in this cab owned a cat.

But a job is a job and I hadn't worked in over three years. You always hope you can make a good movie out of less than stellar material. Sometimes it pays off, and sometimes your endeavor gets a 14% on Rotten Tomatoes.

Nine Lives was about Kevin Spacey becoming a cat. Only his daughter and a "cat whisperer" know the truth about this cat.

"Two out of three boxes," I kept telling myself.

The most attractive part of the deal with EuropaCorp, besides the checked salary box, was Christophe's non-negotiable insistence that Sweetie and I would have to relocate to Paris for six months—box number two.

We flew to France for a preliminary visit to OK the perfect apartment EuropaCorp had rented for our stay. I also scouted the beautiful EuropaCorp stages where I would be filming. Sweetie and I were about to have a life changing adventure—although it would not be the journey we signed up for.

Here's a joke:

The commander of the Sixth Fleet is visiting the captain of the USS *Whatever* when word arrives that Ensign Smith's father has died. The captain calls for all hands on deck and announces to the assembled sailors,

"Ensign Smith, your daddy is dead. Dismissed."

The commander suggests to the captain if anything like that happens again to offer a little more sympathy.

Later that day word arrives that Ensign Smith's mother, overcome with grief, has suffered a massive heart attack and is also deceased.

Once again, the sailors assemble on deck.

The captain, mindful of the commander's advice announces,

"All sailors with a living mother take one step forward.

"Not so fast, Ensign Smith!"

"All those who will be spending the next six months in Paris, France, due to EuropaCorp's non-negotiable demand, take one step forward.

"Not so fast, Ensign Sonnenfeld!"

It turned out filming in Paris cost too much.

We had to shoot the movie in a different French speaking city: Montreal, Canada.

In the winter.

We're now down to one checked box.

The show was green lit because Kevin Spacey agreed to be the lead.

"Those were the days," thinks Kevin.

He must have signed on for the same two out of three checked boxes that were reduced to one when we moved our location from the City of Love to the city of . . . um . . . Montreal. Kevin was not fun to work with. He was mean, unhelpful, critical of other actors, and he had the kind of personality I tried to keep off set as much as possible.

He was dismissive of my friend and fine actor Mark Consuelos, and equally brutal towards Robbie Amell, a Canadian actor he assumed I hired because we needed Canadians. Once he met Robbie, a very handsome young man, Spacey changed his tune.

Kevin was an angry bitchy rotten guy.

Mr. Spacey refused to do ADR until he saw an early edit of the film. After viewing it he insisted we rewrite and reshoot two-thirds of the movie or he would not only refuse to do ADR, he also wouldn't promote the movie. We hired an impersonator to record the lines of ADR dialogue we needed from Kevin.

It was, however, fun to work with Jennifer Garner, Malina Weissman, Mark Consuelos, Robbie Amell, and Cheryl Hines. The following year, I would cast Malina as the lead in *A Series of Unfortunate Events*, for Netflix. Robbie Amell also appeared in a couple of the episodes.

The script called for a "cat whisperer," and we were thrilled when Christopher Walken agreed to be the guy. I took him to lunch at the Hotel Bel-Air to answer any questions about his character, the script, or any other concerns before we met again in Montreal.

At the start of what would be a very short meeting, Chris told me how he worked:

"Look. I'm not actually an actor. I don't need to know about my character's arc, or if my mother was a drunk, or if my daddy beat me. What I do, I go to my weekend place on Block Island. I have a long kitchen table. I spread out the script, all the scenes I'm in, look them over, and I decide who I'm going to imitate. Who my character should sound like. I might decide to impersonate Ethel Merman. Or LBJ. Or Bruce Springsteen. It doesn't matter because I'm a terrible impersonator. You won't know who I'm mimicking, but I will. That's about it."

"Check please," I called to our waiter.

Over the weeks of filming I couldn't get Walken to talk loud enough.

"Hey Chris. That was great. Can we do one more take? Maybe a little louder?"

"Sure."

We'd do another take, and his volume would creep up less than a DB.

"One more. Even louder."

On the last day of Chris' shoot, I told him he really needed to talk much louder. This last scene needed to have some volume.

And this is what Chris Walken said:

"Hey, Barry. There's something I'm not getting."

"What's that, Chris?"

"Aren't I a cat *whisperer*?"

I regret not having a deeper conversation months earlier at the Hotel Bel-Air.

Some advice for studios, producers, and directors: As much as I love working in British Columbia, Canada, with fantastic Vancouver crews, that's how much I deeply, profoundly disliked my Montreal experience. It turns out not all Canadians are nice. The Quebec crew was surly and unprofessional.

The grips and electricians, filthy tool belts strapped to their foie gras infused waists, sat on the "hot set" furniture, which is verboten. A disgruntled crew member threw a bag of cement at my feet.

There was graft, threats, bribes, and intimidation. I don't recommend filming in Montreal. At least not with the crew I was saddled with. In Montreal's defense, Bernard Couture, the lovely Quebecois [which sounds like an oxymoron] cinematographer who filmed a lot of *A Series of Unfortunate Events*, claims there is an excellent "A" and "B" crew in the city, and I got saddled with the "Z" crew. Lucky me.

Since this was a French production, Tierry, the production manager, and Alexandre Bernard, the excellent first assistant director, were brought in from Paris. They hated the Quebecois accent so much they insisted the French speaking crew only speak English.

Jennifer Garner is a beautiful person inside and out. Any time she could, she'd fly back to Los Angeles where she was dealing with her husband, Ben, who was having issues. On her last day of filming, Jennifer was a little off. We were in a grand ballroom with hundreds of extras. I took her to the side of the room and asked if everything was OK.

Behind her, in the distance, were the hundreds of extras.

She apologized for not being at her best. Ben and Jennifer had the night before decided to get a divorce.

I burst into tears.

"It's OK, Barry. It's going to be OK," Jennifer promised.

"How could it be?" I wailed.

"Shhhhh. It's OK. It's going to be OK. It's for the best."

"I don't think so," I howled.

I don't know who was more confused. The 300 extras who wondered what that nice Ms. Garner had said to Mr. Barry to make him so upset, or Jennifer herself who was forced into the role of the calm person after, somehow, I had become the injured party in this discussion.

Montreal had one wonderful thing going for it. Food. The restaurants. The bars. Our local eatery, Le Serpent, riffing on my recipe, created a heavenly spicy margarita which they named, Le Barry.

Maybe the show wasn't a total waste.

Mixing stage. Toronto. A surly Kevin Spacey freeze-frame looks down on Robbie Amell and me.

A Series of Fortunate Events

Being fired off Paramount's *A Series of Unfortunate Events* years earlier was not entirely a downer. I loved the books, but with Scott Rudin leaving the project I didn't look forward to dealing with Jim Carrey without a very strong producer. I also didn't relish the thought of working with Sherry Lansing, a bit of a handful, without having Scott Rudin, my handful, riding shotgun.

Having seen the finished movie, I'm glad Walter Parkes fired me. The Brad Silberling directed version was too Count Olaf/Jimmy Carrey–centric. The three Baudelaire orphans are the strength and driving force of the material, not Count Olaf.

Ten years later, Jimmy Miller told me Netflix had bought the rights to make a streaming version of the show and were looking for a director.

The streamer wanted nothing to do with anyone involved with the movie, and because I was credited as an executive producer, it meant that Netflix wasn't interested in me.

Jimmy convinced the studio I had nothing to do with the feature and got me a meeting. Miller wasn't my manager at the time. Just someone who loved the project and thought I was the right guy for the job.

I walked into the small conference room behind the reception area at Netflix's overburdened offices at 445 Maple Drive. In the meeting were Brian Wright, Teddy Biaselli, and Cindy Holland. As they entered and started to sit, I changed their positions.

"Hiya. Hello. Um, could you sit here. And can you not sit there but instead come over here?"

I wanted to look at the three execs at the same time and not have to turn to my right for some of them and to the left for others. I arranged the team so I was looking left to all three.

"Here's why you should hire me," I rushed into my pitch. "I love the books. I read them to my kid, and when she stopped being interested, I read them for myself. The books and I share the same philosophy. All adults, whether they're villains or have good intentions, are equally ineffectual and dangerous, and all children are capable and smart.

"In addition, here's what we want to do: Shoot the entire show on stage in Vancouver. The sets will be stylized. The acting will be real, though slightly theatrical. And Lemony Snicket will be an on-camera narrator. I don't mean sitting behind a typewriter, like Jude Law did in the movie. I mean walking in and out of scenes."

I knew they were interested in hiring Wes Anderson or Spielberg, so I went on:

"Although the show's tone will be slightly heightened, the viewers must be emotionally invested. They can't simply admire our show, they have to be passionately involved. I'm a fan of Wes Anderson, for instance, but my version will be less twee and more emotional."

I didn't think I had to compare myself to Spielie, since I doubted Netflix would pay what he'd surely demand.

Brian and Teddy asked most of the questions with Cindy keeping her cards close to her vest. Halfway through our very long meeting I realized Cindy was the boss, so I shifted my focus towards her.

I am a devout pessimist but left the meeting knowing I had the job.

The first crew member hired was Bo Welch.

Bo drew up a couple of key set pieces for the show—Briny Beach and Mr. Poe's house and office.

I arranged for a meeting with my three Netflix execs.

Brian, Teddy, and Cindy, as per my instruction, sat on one side of the long conference table. Bo and I sat on the other. My 13-inch MacBook Pro was plugged into the room's 75-inch monitor. The Briny Beach illustration showed a dark gray sky, gloomy sand, and water reflecting a flat, dark, dull environment.

Next up was Mr. Poe's house. Mr. Poe is a penny pincher, and his home reflected his personality. It was a cartoonishly small townhouse with much bigger homes on either side.

The third image also indicated the level of stylization Bo and I intended. It was an illustration of Mr. Poe's office. Poe is a lover of bureaucracy, and the executor of the Baudelaire fortune. Bo designed an extremely narrow, insanely long office whose file cabinets were 11 feet high. It was hilarious, and like all Bo Welch designs, reflected the character who inhabited the space. Teddy and Brian laughed and implied they liked the direction we were headed. Cindy remained silent.

Illustration. Mr. Poe's office.

"Tell me right now if this is the wrong direction because everything else Bo and I are planning is represented by these images. If you don't embrace them, love them, agree with our stylized approach, tell me now, because this represents the tone of the entire series."

"Looks great," said Brian.

"Absolutely," said Teddy.

Cindy remained silent.

Later, I called Brian.

"Hey, Bri: Cindy didn't say a word in there. Is everything OK? This is an expensive undertaking and if Cindy doesn't like it, now's the time to tell me."

"She loves it," said Brian. "She just doesn't think you'll be able to pull it off."

"As long as she likes it," I said.

I was incredibly lucky Netflix suggested I meet Rose Lam, a local Vancouver producer. She was well known and respected in television and made my three years on the project relatively stress free.

From right to left: Rose, llama, and me. Season 1, A Series of Unfortunate Events.

Casting for the most part was easy.

Months earlier Sweetie and I enjoyed a Thanksgiving dinner at Kelly Ripa and Mark Consuelos' house. Among the guests were Neil Patrick Harris, his husband, David, and their two kids. Although I didn't yet have the job, I told Neil I might have a role for him in a few months. Once I was hired, Neil came on board.

Any time I'm directing, I try to find a role for Patrick Warburton. He starred in *The Tick*, was cast as Will Smith's partner in *Men in Black II*, was a cop in *Big Trouble*, and now became Lemony Snicket, the on-screen narrator of *A Series of Unfortunate Events*.

For Violet Baudelaire, the oldest of the three siblings, I cast Malina Weissman, who I had worked with on *Nine Lives*. For Mr. Poe, K. Todd Freeman was the only actor who auditioned with a cough, which the script called for. He got the part and was fantastic.

It is often hard to cast a talented young male actor. Most boys who are in theater tend to be overly theatrical or "Disney-fied." What we needed was someone without artifice or cute theatricality. Malina, who was already hired, came to our last callbacks to read with actors for the role of Klaus Baudelaire, her younger brother. We liked a video we had gotten from Louis Hynes, a kid from Oxford, England, who had put himself on tape. We flew him out to LA. Louis, jet lagged though he was, got the part. With one exception, we had our main cast.

Rose and I knew we needed twins to play young Sunny Baudelaire, the crawling baby sibling of Violet and Klaus. Television shows allow for very limited on set hours for babies, and Sunny was in many, many scenes. That would usually mean hiring twins, as I did for *Addams Family Values*. After Rose, Sweetie, and I auditioned a lot of twins, we ignored prudence and hired nine-month-old Presley, not a twin, but the best actor for the part. She was comedy gold.

The experience I had running *A Series of Unfortunate Events* for Netflix was thrilling and fun. Perhaps it was because Netflix was just getting started producing their original material, but my group of bosses—Teddy, Brian, Ted Sarandos, and especially Cindy Holland, were the most supportive, smartest executives I've worked with.

After I delivered my rough cut of the first two episodes, I was sent an email with Netflix's editing notes. I called Brian Wright and asked if he wanted to see all the requested changes, even if I knew they wouldn't work, or just the edits that could work although not necessarily always better, in my opinion.

Here is what Brian said, which I had never heard before nor since from a studio:

"It's your show. These are just suggestions. Take the ones you like, ignore the ones you don't."

"Well actually, Brian. It's *your* show. Not mine."

"Netflix doesn't see it that way, Barry. It's your show."

A Series of Unfortunate Events received a Peabody Award and was nominated each of its three years for an Emmy. Bo received multiple nominations for his production design, and Rita Ciccozzi and Julie McHaffie, our hair and makeup team, won several awards. Bo and Alan Arkush each received a Directors Guild of America nomination for directing, and I received three nominations.

Sweetie and I rented a wonderful apartment on the 52nd floor of the Shangri-La Hotel in downtown Vancouver, our view encompassing English Bay and Coal Harbor. Every other weekend either Rose and her husband, Todd Elyzen, or the Sonnenfelds would have parties for the cast and key members of the crew. These parties were famous for brutally shaken Belvedere vodka martinis or my spicy jalapeño margaritas.

Sweetie was on set every day and was a second pair of eyes, with Rose being another set. We had two wonderful, talented cameramen—Bernard Couture, the nicest Quebecois I've ever met, and Rose's husband, Todd, who had a very sharp sense of humor. Unlike any studio I've worked for, Netflix had given me true authorship. Having come off *Men in Black 3*, where Amy Pascal commandeered the cutting room, insisting an over the shoulder shot become a close-up, and demanding I use a take where Will Smith doesn't shed a tear for his dead father, Netflix treated me with dignity and respect.

Me, Warburton, and Sweetie the photo bomber during one of our parties. Me with spicy margarita. Warburton with brutally shaken Belvedere vodka.

A *Series of Unfortunate Events* was my first experience as a show runner. Brian Wright originally hired me to direct the pilot and be a supervising executive producer, possibly directing other episodes over the planned three years. Someone else had been hired as the show runner—a person, usually a writer, who is in charge of everything, including tone. It very quickly became apparent to both Brian and me that Netflix had hired the wrong guy. Brian asked if I was willing to take over show running on top of my other duties, and I absolutely embraced it.

As a director, I didn't always appreciate on-set interference from producers—yet here I was, the producer/show runner, asking a series of directors to copy my tone and pace. My marching orders to our directors was simple: fast and flat.

I tried to stay off the set as much as possible so neither the director nor I would be frustrated. I know how hard directing is, and I also know how much of a pushy know-it-all I am. I trusted Rose, who embraced my tone, to keep watch over our episodic directors.

Malina, our Violet Baudelaire, told me she always knew I had come down to the set, even without seeing me, because the director would come up to the cast and say, "Let's do one more, a lot faster."

All studios should copy the early Netflix philosophy: Take your time finding the best director or show runner for your project, trust that you hired the right person, and let that person be in charge. No studio exec is telling their dentist or heart surgeon what tool to use, nor their plumber which screw to unfasten first, yet almost every studio executive, no matter how new to the craft, thinks they know how to direct.

Who Are You and Why Are You Here?

I was directing "The Wide Window" episodes of *A Series of Unfortunate Events*, late in October 2016. Alfre Woodard was the guest star.

A quick Alfre story:

Neil Patrick Harris told me that Alfre called him after the first week and asked:

"Does Barry give you direction?"

"Sure," said NPH.

"And do you follow it?"

"Absolutely."

"I do too. But I'm not sure why."

We had a closed set, which meant non-crew members were not allowed on stage without a special invitation. This day there was a sporty woman and her kid on set. I was making fun of her, and she was giving back as good as I gave. She had shortish hair and a feisty attitude. At some point between setups, I asked:

"Who are you and why are you here?"

"I'm here because my son loves the books and asked me to get us on your set.

"As for who I am, I'm Christy Clark," she said as she offered up her hand for shaking, "premier of British Columbia."

"You might be very important to me in the next couple of weeks," is all I said.

Two weeks later, early the morning of November 9, 2016, I received an email from Christy:

"Are you ready?"

Trump had won the US presidential election and Christy was offering me a lifeline.

As you may remember from my chapter on Donald Trump, I was among those who knew what a sociopath he was even before he took office.

"Hire an immigration lawyer and start the process," she emailed.

Sweetie and I had spent enough time working in Canada, in both Vancouver and unfortunately Montreal, that we were eligible for permanent residency status.

Ms. Clark knew it had been my choice to bring *A Series of Unfortunate Events* to Canada, which employed a minimum of 350 crew members a week. British Columbia was sure to benefit from my personal interest in Canada.

"Who do you know?" my lawyer asked. "This process should take fourteen months and it looks like it will wrap up in six weeks."

"Christy Clark?" I guessed.

"That'll do it," he said.

Conscious Narcissistic Rage

Sweetie and I were in Los Angeles visiting Chloe, our youngest daughter. We were staying at the Maybourne in Beverly Hills, and were on South Beverly Drive, walking back to our hotel having chosen the non-room-service breakfast option. Coming towards us were my manager, Jimmy Miller, and his friend, I guess, Mel Gibson.

"Hey Ba."

"Hey Jimmy. You know Sweetie."

"Sure. And you know Mel, right?"

"Yeah, we've met," says Mel, who looked slightly like a homeless guy this morning.

"Where are you guys going?" I ask for some stupid reason, as if it was any of my business.

"I'm taking Mel to my physical therapist," offers Jimmy. "He's got really bad sciatica."

Being the sciatica GOAT, I offer:

"You can go to Jimmy's PT guy, Mel, but the issue isn't physical. It's mental.

"Your problem is you have unconscious narcissistic rage."

I thought about that remark for only half a second before contradicting myself:

"What am I talking about? Your rage isn't unconscious."

Luckily Jimmy, Sweetie, and most importantly Mel, got the joke.

On How I Almost Got Fired Before I Even Started Directing My First Musical

In early December 2019, my talent agency sent me the scripts for *Schmigadoon!*, a musical comedy written by Cinco Paul and produced by Broadway Video, Lorne Michaels' production company.

Sweetie, Bo, and Rose read the scripts.

The triad said I should do it. They thought it was fun, funny, and we could film it on stage in Vancouver. I wasn't sure. I hated musicals.

Singin' in the Rain I could tolerate due to Donald O'Connor's dance number "Make 'Em Laugh." I also loved the music and shooting style of *Hair* and *Pennies from Heaven*. I will admit I sang "Every Sperm Is Sacred," a wonderful number from *Monty Python's The Meaning of Life*, to baby Chloe while rocking her to sleep, but I was being ironic. Most nights I preferred singing a lullaby version of "Eve of Destruction."

Because I wanted to keep working with Bo and Rose, and because Sweetie said I should do it, on Friday, January 13, 2020, I took a video conference call with Andrew Singer, president of Broadway Video; Micah Frank and Caroline Maloney, two more Broadway Video execs; and Cinco Paul, the creator of the series.

I told the Zoomers I hated musicals, but knew how to direct them, which was to film the dance numbers in long, wide shots showing the actor's entire body instead of a *Flashdance*, or a Rob

Marshall, style of filming, which was to edit the sequence into many quick cuts [I actually suggested they hire Rob Marshall]. I also said none of the actors should acknowledge they're in a musical or a comedy. If they played the scenes straight and not for laughs—and talked fast—we'd be fine.

The call went well enough that two weeks later, I flew to New York to meet Lorne Michaels.

Lorne is a power whisperer, talking very quietly, forcing you to lean in, almost bow to hear him speak. He is many things I am not. He is strategic and keeps his cards close to his vest. I am loud, guileless, and often don't read my audience. I have an allergic reaction to authority, which is particularly difficult since I live to be in charge. This internal conflict is resolved through self-loathing.

In the fall of 2020, during the Covid-19 pandemic, Rose and I convinced Universal and Apple TV+ that we could make *Schmigadoon!* entirely on stage in Vancouver with enough precautions that Covid wouldn't shut us down.

On set wearing a mask, goggles, Cuban smoking hat, and an Etro scarf Sweetie says makes me look like Barbara Corcoran.

Universal was extremely skeptical. And often unhelpful. At the time, very few shows were in production. With a Canadian two-week quarantine, daily Covid testing procedures, on-set safety rules, and the risk of financial calamity if any of our actors caught the disease, it took all of Rose's and my substantial pushiness to get the project green lit.

A week before filming, with our large and talented cast isolating in various hotel rooms, rental apartments, and houses throughout Vancouver, Universal arranged for a Zoom call with its HR department to let the actors and producers know how the studio expected us to behave.

Yes, I know I should have muted my mic, turned off the computer's camera, and taken a three-hour nap while the call droned on. Instead, I did the opposite.

It goes back to that authority thing.

Hours into the Zoom session, the HR moderator presented the *Hollywood Squares'* worth of boxed faces with the following theoretical:

You are sitting at your desk. It is during the crew's lunch hour. No one is in the production office, but in the distance you see two electricians at the water cooler. You overhear one friend ask the other if he had seen Chris Rock's monologue on that weekend's Saturday Night Live. *His buddy says he hadn't.*

The first guy proceeds to tell his friend, in the empty room except for you, about Chris' monologue. They laugh together as the electrician who had seen the show repeats in graphic detail, Chris' speech. The electrician quotes verbatim, very specific words and phrases that could be construed to be offensive.

The moderator asked our little Zoom squares what we should do.

"Do nothing!" I declare.

"Excuse me?" said the incredulous moderator.

"You said it was two friends in an empty room. You said I *OVER-HEAR* their conversation. It's none of my business. I have no right, *OVERHEARING* two pals on their *LUNCH BREAK*, to get involved. Besides, whatever the offensive nature of the monologue might have been, it didn't offend *me* and I'm the only other person in the room."

"Is that how the rest of you feel?" asked the moderator.

A sing-songy-teacher's-pet voice spoke up: "You approach the electricians and tell them their discussion is not appropriate for the workplace and ask them to refrain from that kind of talk."

"That's right," said the moderator.

Suddenly I'm in 2nd grade.

I found myself saying:

"That makes no sense. Who am I to tell them what they can talk about on their lunch hour. You said they were friends. You said no one was in the room. They were enjoying their conversation. It is *NONE OF MY BUSINESS.*"

That evening I was in my office on the Vancouver film lot when Jimmy Miller, my manager, called. Jimmy will always tell the truth.

"Ba. Don't get angry. Just listen. OK?"

"Oh, God. I know what this is about."

"Let me get through this with you, OK?"

"Go."

"I got a call from the chairman of the studio. She told me what you said on the call."

"Yeah, but . . ."

"Let me say this."

"Yup."

"They have agreed not to fire you."

"Fire me? You can't be serious."

"They aren't going to."

"Well, yeah, based on what could they fire me?"

"Ba."

"OK. I'll shut up."

"They're not going to fire you as long as you agree to go to every actor on that Zoom, individually, and tell them how important it is they feel safe. That if anything upsets them, or makes them uncomfortable, they know they can come to you. That nothing is more important to you than having your actors feel like they're protected."

"Well of course I feel that way. But Jimmy. The studio's scenario was two guys at a water cooler and me *OVERHEARING* their Chris Rock monologue conversation, which by the way, was broadcast by NBC, owned by Universal, to probably ten million people. There was no disclaimer stating *'We hope Chris doesn't offend anyone with his monologue, but please call this 800 number if you're feeling uncomfortable.'* This makes no sense!"

"Do it, Ba. Go to every actor on that call and let them know, in all sincerity, that you want them to feel safe."

Over the next week, as each actor came out of quarantine and appeared on our set for the first time, I would take them aside:

"I want you to know how important it is that you feel safe and secure on the set and if at any point you see or hear anything that makes you uncomfortable, in any way, please come to me immediately and I will fix it."

Because none of the actors knew why I was saying this, they would laugh and say a version of "You got it, Ba."

When one of the female leads of *Schmigadoon!*, an actor I had directed many times, showed up for her first day, I took her aside: "I want you to know how important it is that you feel safe and secure on set and if at any point you see or hear anything that makes you uncomfortable, please come to me immediately and I will remedy the situation."

"Suck my dick," said Kristin Chenoweth.

I love her.

Kristin Chenoweth, 2006.

Magic Hour

On a Saturday evening, early April 2012, nearing completion of *Men in Black 3*, I found myself alone on the magical SONY lot in Culver City. I had come in late that afternoon to listen to some last-minute sound effects Paul Ottosson, the three-time Academy Award winning sound designer, was proposing as "sweeteners" for some of the alien voices. After our meeting, I walked around the lot by myself.

To get onto the lot and into various stages, facilities, and executive office buildings, one needed an electronic badge with a photo. My badge was unique—the only one in SONY's modern history of a person wearing a hat—my signature, slightly asshole-ish, cowboy hat.

A year earlier when I started *MIB3* the security office photographer told me no photos with hats. I started to remove my custom made [I have a pinhead] white cowboy hat.

That's when one of the security guys stopped me.

"Let's check on that."

I've always been friendly to the security staff. The guards have a terrible job dealing with entitled, empowered shitheads. I embraced being a shithead, but only to those who were in positions of power greater than me.

"What's that going to entail?" I asked.

"We just need to check with Gary."

"Gary Martin? Maybe he has better things . . ."

"It'll just take a second."

Gary, as the president of physical production, ran the entire SONY campus. He suffered no fools.

"Hey, guys. I'm not sure my wearing a hat is worthy of Gary's time."

Too late. The question was asked.

"Let the Little Shit wear his cowboy hat," Gary boomed over the speaker phone.

It was magic hour. The sun had set but there was still light in the sky—deep blue with hints of magenta and deep orange. The white water tower with its cold blue neon SONY sign loomed over the lot. Using my all-access cowboy-hatted badge, I wandered onto different stages and strolled down the main thoroughfare of SONY Pictures, eventually letting myself in to the side entrance of the Thalberg Building, which housed the offices of all the studio execs I had worked with on four SONY movies over the past 17 years.

To paraphrase Scott Rudin: If I couldn't be happy today, my mother won.

If someone had told me my career would have super highs and devastating lows—that in addition to marrying the woman of my dreams, the biggest surprise of all—I'd have a career in the actual film business, becoming a cinematographer, director, and producer, able to walk anywhere I wanted on an actual studio lot, at magic hour, in Hollywood, with a one of a kind cowboy hat badge? Here's what I would say:

"Whatever you do, don't open Schrödinger's box. This reality is pretty great."

Acknowledgments

To Sweetie. Your love and support during the good half of my life has given me the strength and clarity to deal with the bad half.

Thank you to everyone at Hachette books for helping me frame, edit, and distribute my two books. Hopefully there will be more.

Directors get all the blame for flops, and all the credit for successes. Any success I have achieved is due to the grips, electricians, property masters, costume designers, hair and makeup artists, editors, DPs, production designers, assistant directors, production assistants, writers, sound mixers, teamsters, wonderful actors, and some [but not all] producers who made me look good. I've been lucky to work with many of the best crews in the industry.

Finally, I recognize the role luck has played in my life. If I hadn't met Joel Coen at a party, hadn't let Scott Rudin talk me into directing when I was a happy cinematographer, if I hadn't produced documentaries for Elliott Erwitt, hadn't met Susan Ringo, and hadn't picked more good scripts than bad, I'd be somewhere other than where I am today, wherever that is. Thank you, Luck.

Photo Credits

All photographs and images courtesy of the author with the following exceptions: